The Overcoming BLOOD

BOB LAMB

Whitaker House

THE OVERCOMING BLOOD

Bob Lamb
7138 S. Darlington
Tulsa, OK 74136

ISBN: 0-88368-270-2
Printed in the United States of America
Copyright© 1993 by Whitaker House

Whitaker House
580 Pittsburgh Street
Springdale, PA 15144

The
Overcoming
BLOOD

Contents

Introduction

Introduction

A Foundation

For years my faith was in God, Jesus, the Holy Spirit and the Bible in a general sort of way. When searching for a more specific basis for my faith, I discovered strong biblical reasons to place my faith in the blood of Jesus Christ. Now my faith is based on a fundamental aspect of God's provision for us—the blood of Jesus. The blood is a solid foundation for developing powerful faith.

More than a Ritual

For years I participated regularly in the communion service, but I didn't fully understand what I was doing. It seemed all I got out of it were the words, *"This do in remembrance of me"* and *"For as often as you eat this bread, and drink this cup, you do show the Lord's death till he come"* (1 Corinthians 11:24-26).

I had always looked backward in time to the cross by *"remembrance"* and forward in time to the rapture by *"till he come."* I never looked to the present moment, the time in which I was taking the bread and the cup.

Intuitively, I knew that correctly partaking of the Lord's supper should result in something more than a mental exercise of looking backward and forward in time. I felt communion should benefit every Christian personally.

I searched the Scriptures to discover what was lacking in my understanding of this fundamental ordinance of the church. In doing so, I discovered three key concepts that have helped me immensely. These discoveries are the basis for this book.

When Jesus instituted the Lord's supper, He did so with references to the Passover, the blood covenant, and the kingdom of God. These are examined in Biblical detail to provide an understanding of the reasons we may expect miracles and healings to occur when we partake of the Lord's table.

Pleading the Blood

A study of the blood of Jesus yields very sound answers to the question, "What does it mean to 'plead the blood'?" Jesus' blood is alive and speaks on our behalf today. Many examples from the Bible show the relationship between the blood of Jesus and a particular benefit such as redemption, forgiveness of sins, cleansing, sanctification, and healing. When we plead the blood, it is a valid, scriptural expression of our faith in that blood.

PART ONE:

The Blood of Jesus, A Foundation for Faith

Chapter 1

These Three

*But now abide faith, hope, love, these three;
but the greatest of these is love.*
—*1 Corinthians 13:13* NAS

I have often meditated on this concluding verse of the great love chapter of 1 Corinthians. Recently, a new insight came while considering faith, hope, and love.

I began asking myself, "What if I went around saying to myself and to those around me, 'I have hope, I have hope, I have hope...'?"

Wouldn't someone say, "Bob, what do you have hope in? What is the object of your hope?"

Or, what if I said "I have love, I have love, I have love..." everywhere I went?

Again, it wouldn't be long before someone would say, "What or whom do you love? What is the object of your love?"

I say this because I do say to myself and to those around me, "I have faith, I have faith, I have faith!" Yet, when I say this, no one questions me about the object of my faith. It seems that everyone, myself included, knows what I mean when I say, "I have faith."

One day the insight came that I was operating under a double standard. I was requiring hope to have an object. I was requiring love to have an object. But I didn't require faith to have an object.

What I am about to relate developed while reflecting on faith, hope, and love. It is not a complete revelation, and I am not attempting to set doctrine. But it has helped me to have an object for my faith.

Elephants

What I will share reminds me of the story of six blindfolded men standing around a large cage. Unknown to them, the cage encloses a huge elephant. They are told to reach inside and describe the unknown creature by what they feel. Of course, the story is funny as each person perceives and describes what the creature is based solely on the particular part he handles. The descriptions range from interpretations of a long rope (the tail), to a gigantic palm leaf (an ear), to a flexible water hose (the trunk).

Likewise, what I am going to describe is just one facet of faith. It is not by any means the whole picture. But just as knowledge of an elephant's trunk is necessary to have a complete understanding of an elephant, I believe what I am going to describe will help us to better understand faith.

Before I get to objects of faith, let me first consider some objects of hope and love.

Objects of Our Hope

Let me begin by giving some scriptural examples of hope having an object:

27Christ in you, the hope of glory.
                    (Colossians 1:27)

1Lord Jesus Christ, which is our hope.
                    (1 Timothy 1:1)

13Looking for that blessed hope, and the glorious appearing of the great God and our Savior Jesus Christ.   (Titus 2:13)

All of these Scriptures point to Jesus as the object of hope. Of course, many Scriptures mention hope without an object. The opening verse of 1 Corinthians 13:13, taken out of context, is perhaps the most familiar. Not all scriptural references on hope tell us explicitly what the object of that hope should be. Nevertheless, there are sufficient verses to encourage us to direct our hope toward a specific object.

Consequently, I don't go around anymore saying to myself and others, "I have hope, I have hope, I have hope..." like a broken record. Instead, I give my hope an object. I can now paraphrase the above Scriptures as: "Christ is in me, the hope of glory," "The Lord Jesus Christ is my hope," and "I look for that blessed hope and the glorious appearing of my God and Savior, Jesus Christ." Thus, knowing the object of my hope and giving that hope a focal point strengthens the very foundation of it.

Objects of Our Love

Here are three scriptural examples of love with an object:

> *⁹Eye hath not seen, nor ear heard, neither have entered into the heart of man, the things which God hath prepared for them that love Him.* *(1 Corinthians 2:9)*

> *¹⁴The love of Christ constraineth us.* *(2 Corinthians 5:14)*

> *¹⁹Husbands, love your wives, and be not bitter against them.* *(Colossians 3:19)*

These three verses express different objects for love. Again, many verses speak of love without an object. It is just that I am greatly helped by having an object for my love.

Now my love focuses on objects. That is, instead of saying, "I have love, I have love, I have love...," I now paraphrase Scriptures by saying, "I pray to know the love of Christ that I might be filled with all the fullness of God" (Ephesians 3:19), and "As a husband, I love my wife" (Colossians 3:19).

If I simply say, "I have love," the focus is on myself and my ability to love. However, if I say, "I love my wife," I begin to focus more on the object of my love (my wife). Then my love has a direction to flow. It is then that my love becomes more believable to both myself and the object of my love. Consequently, these positive statements of focusing on objects of my hope and of my love make hope and love much more real to me.

Objects of Our Faith

Real help came to me by applying this same understanding to the principle of faith. If hope and love have objects, then I knew within me that faith must also have objects. While it is true to say, "I have faith," my understanding was really helped to know the object of my faith.

What should be the object of my faith? What should I concentrate on? I immediately thought of God, Jesus, the Holy Spirit, and the Word of God. With good scriptural reasons, too! I considered verses such as:

²²Have faith in God.   *(Mark 11:22)*

²⁶For ye are all the children of God by faith in Christ Jesus.
      (Galatians 3:26)

⁹To another faith by the same Spirit.
      (1 Corinthians 12:9)

¹⁷So then faith cometh by hearing, and hearing by the word of God.
      (Romans 10:17)

God, Jesus Christ, the Holy Spirit, and the Word are indeed objects for my faith as shown in these Scriptures. But I needed a more bite-sized object—that is, an object that I could focus on more sharply.

As long as I could neither direct my faith nor see its object, I would be less likely to even use that faith. But if I knew exactly what my faith was in, that faith would become a more effective weapon in my spiritual arsenal.

Consider a soldier. If a weapon is placed in his hands which he has never been trained to use, he won't be able to use it effectively. He wouldn't know how to aim, fire or maintain it properly. He would lack the knowledge of its strengths or its weaknesses. Thus, the weapon would not be an asset to him. In the same way, a spiritual weapon that we don't fully appreciate or understand is of little help to us.

What my spirit seemed to require was a specific attribute of God as revealed in the Word. What would the object of my faith be? Would it be one of the three "textbook" attributes of God—His omniscience (all knowing), His omnipresence (everywhere present), His omnipotence (all powerful)? Would it be His holiness, His creative ability, His kingdom? The choices seemed endless.

The Search

The familiar verse of *"without faith it is impossible to please him"* (Hebrews 11:6) was ever before me as I considered faith. I found myself asking, "Faith in what?" or "Faith in whom?"

Part of the answer came when I considered that the Bible is the very source for knowledge of God. *"The Word was made flesh, and dwelt among us"* (John 1:14) equates the living Word with the written Word in the Person of Jesus Christ. That is, to read, study, and meditate in

17

the Word is to know God. His very personality is revealed in the Bible because the written Word and the living Word are one in the same!

I was greatly helped to realize this truth. I now mentally made an addition to Hebrews 11:6 every time I thought about it. I now said, "Without faith in the Word of God it is impossible to please Him." The object of my faith at this point was the written Word. "If God said it, I believe it, it is so" was my motto. Then one day it dawned on me that if God said it, it was so whether or not I believed it! "If God said it, it is so" became my shortened motto.

This approach to developing our faith is 100 percent correct. For we read in Romans 10:17, *so then faith cometh by hearing, and hearing by the Word of God."* Our faith comes and is developed by hearing the Word of God. The word *"hearing"* certainly includes reading and meditating on the Word.

I then began saying to myself and to others, "I have faith in the Word of God. The object of my faith is the Word of God." Those around me nodded their heads in approval for they understood, as I did, in a general way what I meant.

Yet my spirit still seemed to be unsettled. I found myself calculating, "My Bible has some 1,200 pages. There are more than 23,000 verses in the Old Testament and nearly 8,000 verses in the New Testament. That means nearly

750,000 words to consider. At an average of five letters to a word, that is almost four million letters! What can I do to make all this material more manageable?" My faith in the Word still seemed too general to be effective.

So in an effort to zero in on the very foundations upon which the Word is based, I began asking myself, "What, then, is the most important revelation in the New Testament?" I continued my search.

Of First Importance

When asking the Lord about these things, I was immediately led to the answer. It is found in 1 Corinthians 15:3-4:

> *³For what I received I passed on to you as of first importance: that Christ died for our sins according to the Scriptures, ⁴that he was buried, that he was raised on the third day according to the Scriptures.*
>
> *(NIV)*

Christ's death, burial, and resurrection are called *"of first importance."* I found great release in finding this revelation of truth. Why do I call this a *"revelation"*? Because the Apostle Paul did! In writing to Christians in the churches in Galatia, he says:

> *[11]The gospel which was preached of me is not after man.*
> *[12]For I neither received it of man, neither was I taught it, but by the revelation of Jesus Christ.*   (Galatians 1:11-12)

"That Christ died for our sins" is the part of the revelation that is preached and taught most frequently. And it is here that the Holy Spirit impressed upon me to study and meditate on this event *"of first importance."*

As I meditated on the fact of Christ's dying for our sins, a deeper meaning regarding the blood of Jesus began to unfold. Could it be the blood of Jesus would become the object, the foundation for my faith?

Chapter 2

The Blood of Jesus

In whom we have redemption through his blood, the forgiveness of sins, according to the riches of his grace.
—Ephesians 1:7

A tremendous area of revelation exists in the study of the blood of Jesus. A deeper understanding of what it means to "plead the blood" of Jesus Christ came as a result of studying the Word about His blood.

I found many very specific Scriptures that reveal what the blood of Jesus Christ has provided for us. The list grew and grew. To discover that so many different provisions for our benefit are embodied in the shed blood of our Lord Jesus Christ is truly amazing. I will list some of these provisions with a key verse for each one. Notice that each verse states that the blood of Jesus Christ is the basis or the reason why we as Christians possess these benefits.

REDEMPTION: *Ye were...redeemed... with the precious blood of Christ.*
(1 Peter 1:18-19)

FORGIVENESS OF SINS: *Without the shedding of blood there is no forgiveness.*
(Hebrews 9:22 NIV)

CLEANSING: *The blood of Jesus Christ his Son cleanseth us from all sin.*
(1 John 1:7)

JUSTIFICATION: *Being now justified by his blood.*
(Romans 5:9)

RECONCILIATION: *For God set him before the world, to be, by the shedding of his blood, a means of reconciliation through faith.*
(Romans 3:25 TCNT)

SANCTIFICATION: *Jesus also, that he might sanctify the people with his own blood, suffered without the gate.*
(Hebrews 13:12)

PEACE: *And, having made peace through the blood of his cross.*
(Colossians 1:20)

APPROACH TO GOD: *Having therefore, brethren, boldness to enter into the holiest by the blood of Jesus.*
(Hebrews 10:19)

ETERNAL INHERITANCE: *By his own blood he entered in once into the holy place, having obtained eternal redemption for us.* (Hebrews 9:12)

The blood of Jesus is mentioned explicitly in connection with each of the above benefits it has provided for us. In addition, the blood of Jesus is mentioned implicitly in many other Scriptures. For example, the fact that the blood provides for our physical healing is implicit in the Scripture:

HEALING: *By whose stripes ye were healed.* (1 Peter 2:24)

Clearly, this verse implies that Jesus' blood was shed for our healing. This short statement, therefore, gives us a basis for our physical healing, the blood of Jesus Christ.

The point I am making by listing these verses is that the blood of Jesus is linked to each benefit. That is, all the provisions of Christ's dying for us are directly related to His blood. They are ours when we confess Jesus as our Lord and believe that God raised Him from the dead (Romans 10:9-10).

In other words, acceptance of these Scriptures accomplishes two very powerful results. One, our faith grows (Romans 10:17); and two, we recognize the object of that faith.

It is the blood of Jesus Christ that purchased our salvation with all the associated benefits. When we understand this, our faith in the blood of Jesus Christ soars to new heights. This revelation is why I came to the understanding that the object, the foundation of my faith is the blood of Jesus Christ.

Is It Scriptural?

It is one thing to believe and appreciate what the blood has accomplished for us. It is another thing to place our faith in the blood of Jesus if the Bible is silent about doing so. In other words, is it scriptural to say that our faith is in the blood of Jesus Christ? Does the Bible ever make such a statement?

I am aware of the Scripture passage which clearly states:

> [5]That your faith should not stand in the wisdom of men, but in the power of God.
> (1 Corinthians 2:5)

Faith in the power of God! Yes, my faith does stand in the power of God. Most every time I praise God for His marvelous deeds, I naturally recall His power. I think of His immense creation. I think of His opening the Red Sea for some 2.5 million Israelites to pass safely through while their pursuers were drowned. I think of His stopping the sun in response to Joshua's prayer. And I always think of the power of God raising Jesus from the dead. Yes, my faith is in the power of God. No problem.

Then, too I am aware of Acts 3:16 where the man crippled from birth was healed by faith in the name of Jesus. The verse plainly reads:

> [16]By faith in the name of Jesus, this man whom you see and know was made strong.
> (NIV)

Faith in the name of Jesus healed a life-long cripple! Yes, my faith is also in the name of Jesus Christ. Again, no problem.

However, my spirit seemed to require faith in Jesus Christ and, in particular, faith in His blood. But is it scriptural? Let me show how I arrived at the discovery that faith in the blood of Jesus Christ is indeed set forth in the New Testament.

Chapter 3

Faith and Blood

*Whom God hath set forth to be a propitiation
through faith in His blood.*
—Romans 3:25

Chapters three, four, and five of Romans
lay a mighty foundation for the truth of
righteousness by faith in the blood of Jesus.

Through Martin Luther, German leader of
the Protestant Reformation, God restored the
truth of justification by faith. Luther's questions were the same as yours and mine: How
does a man find favor with God? Do we find
favor by more prayers, more fasting, more
works? No, God's favor is not a prize to be won,
but a gift to be accepted.

Another way of saying this is that God
makes men righteous before Him, not through
man's moral goodness or his good works, but
because of God's kindness to them. His kindness was given to the world in the life, death,
and resurrection of Jesus Christ. A true
acceptance of God's kindness results in man's

being declared righteous (Romans 10:9-10). This is the meaning of justification by faith.

Groundwork

Let me give dictionary definitions of these scriptural terms that will help us understand these mighty truths:

RIGHTEOUSNESS: *the quality or state of being righteous, just, or rightful.*

JUSTIFICATION: *the act of God whereby man is absolved of guilt for sin.*

PROPITIATION: *to make favorably inclined; conciliate; appease.*

My search led me to Romans. I found that I am justified, I am made righteous by faith. Again, however, I found myself asking, "Faith in what? Faith in whom? What is the object of my faith?"

The study of Romans showed me the object of my faith would be Jesus Christ. But questions kept nagging me: "What is it about Jesus that I should place my faith in? Should my faith be grounded in His virgin birth? In His holy life? In the miracles He performed?"

Each one of these attributes of Jesus is certainly true and worthy to be an object of faith. But yet I kept going back to 1 Corinthians 15:3-4. There it says that the death, burial, and resurrection of Jesus Christ are *"of first importance."* I knew within my spirit that my answer would be found in one of these events.

Discovery

I well remember the day when I discovered the scriptural verification of faith in the blood of Jesus. I had turned to Romans and began to summarize the book by reading just the topical headings that my Bible has at the beginning of every chapter and many times within chapters. I had glanced through the topics of "The Power of the Gospel," "The Guilt of Mankind," and so on until I reached chapter three. There as a caption to verse 21, was the heading, "Righteousness through Faith." I then began reading very carefully, looking to see if the Word would reveal whether "Righteousness through Faith" would have an object. Again, I knew my faith was already based on Jesus Christ as my Savior and Lord. This was an expression of my faith in a general way. My search was to find a specific attribute of Jesus in which to place my faith.

The discovery came as I was reading verse 25. The words *"faith in His blood"* jumped off the page into my spirit. This was the answer I was looking for! The object of my faith can indeed be the blood of Jesus Christ.

I admit I reached for the dictionary to see what the word *propitiation* means. It means that God was favorably inclined, conciliated, or appeased through sending forth Jesus into the world to die for us. He then is our redemption through *"faith in His blood."*

The truths revealed in Romans 3:21-26 satisfied what I was looking for. Let me paraphrase these verses as I read them that day:

> [21]Jesus, the righteousness of God, was manifested in the flesh as foretold.
> [22]This righteousness of God comes to us by faith in Jesus Christ.
> [23]Our sin nature separated us from God.
> [24]We are justified freely by the grace of God. How? Through the redemption that came by Jesus Christ.
> [25]How did the redemption come? God set Jesus to be a propitiation (Jesus turned aside God's wrath by taking upon Himself our sinful nature). How are we to receive this redemption? **Through faith in His blood.**
> [26]We all acknowledge God is just. So are all who believe in Jesus.
>
> (author's paraphrase)

Each one of these verses is so rich! Verse 25 was the one, taken in context, that provided the answer I was seeking.

Redemption is through faith in what? Faith in Jesus' virgin birth? While I believe Jesus was born of a virgin, verse 25 says redemption isn't by faith in His virgin birth. Faith in the miracles Jesus performed while on earth? I do believe every account of every miracle recorded in the Word. However, verse 25 says our redemption is not to be by faith in Jesus' miracles. Faith in Jesus' holy life, that He lived under the very rigorous Old Testament law and yet never sinned? I believe He did, but verse 25 says our faith for redemption lies elsewhere.

In what do I place my faith for redemption? Scripture says it very plainly—*"faith in His blood"*! This is what I was seeking. The Bible verifies the blood of Jesus Christ is the object, the foundation of my faith.

Chapter 4

More Witnesses

*Therefore being **justified by faith,**
we have peace with God through
our Lord Jesus Christ.*
—Romans 5:1

*Much more then, being now **justified
by his blood,** we shall be saved
from wrath through him.*
—Romans 5:9

For God to justify us (Romans 3:26) would mean we would be in His sight as if we had never sinned. For God to justify us would make us like Adam and Eve before they fell in the Garden of Eden. If we had never sinned, we would be in perfect fellowship with God. However, because we have sinned, we need to look deeper into the meaning of God's powerful provision of justification.

Our text verses state we are justified by faith and by His blood. If someone would ask us how can we possibly say that God has justified us (as if we had never sinned), we could say, *"by faith"* (Romans 5:1). If someone else would ask us the same question, we could answer him, *"by His blood"* (Romans 5:9). Very good. We have given two different answers to the same question! And both are the truth from God's Word.

Let us say the same thing another way. Suppose you know the meaning of the word *justification* and you ask yourself, "How am I justified?" You can find in Romans 5:1 that it is *"by faith"* and in Romans 5:9 that it is *"by His blood."* What conclusion do you come to? Certainly, it is not either/or but both! We can say, "I am justified by faith in His blood."

Justification by Faith in Jesus' Blood

This conclusion is a good example of what I am trying to show. Using the first verse, I would confess the truth that "I am justified by faith." Here the word *faith* has no object. Taken by itself, I really don't have a good concept of what I have faith in so that I can *"have peace with God through our Lord Jesus Christ"* (Romans 5:1). However, taken in context with the previous chapter which deals with Abraham's righteousness because of his faith in God's promise, we see that our righteousness is obtained *"if we believe on him that raised up Jesus our Lord from the dead"* (Romans 4:24). Abraham believed in God's spoken Word; we believe in God's written Word.

The word *"therefore"* in Romans 5:1 links our believing to our *"being justified by faith."* The fact of Jesus being raised from the dead certainly implies He had shed His blood. Hence, taken in context, we are justified by faith in His blood.

Using the Romans 5:9 verse, I would confess the truth "I am justified by his blood." Here again, taken in context, we are justified by his blood because *"God commended his love toward us, in that, while we were yet sinners, Christ died for us"* (verse 8). Again, Scripture explicitly links the death of Christ with His blood.

The justification that both verses speak about is based on Christ's dying for us. So our justification is by faith, and the object of our faith is the blood of Jesus Christ.

Blood Everywhere

Now I see the blood of Jesus everywhere in Scripture. Every time the death, burial, or resurrection of Jesus is mentioned (*"of first importance"*), I see His blood.

For example, consider the best-known verse in the Bible:

> *¹⁶For God so loved the world, that he gave his only begotten Son, that whosoever believeth in him should not perish, but have everlasting life.   (John 3:16)*

I see in the word *"gave"* the implied shedding of His blood. I see in the word *"believe"* the equivalent of the word *"faith."* (*Believe* is the verb, and *faith* is the noun of the same Greek root word.) So my faith for *"everlasting life"* is based on the shed blood of Jesus Christ.

Another example is Romans 8:32. I call this the companion verse to John 3:16:

> *³²He that spared not his own Son, but delivered him up for us all, how shall he not with him also freely give us all things?   (Romans 8:32)*

Again, I see in the words *"spared not"* and *"delivered him up for us all"* His blood being shed for us.

How do we appropriate what the last part of the verse so wondrously promises? For me, it is by faith in His blood that makes each word so very powerful in itself. Consider the meaning of each word of that last phrase separately:

HOW — God will
SHALL — a very strong word
HE NOT — our Father will
WITH HIM — with Jesus
ALSO — besides *"born again"*
FREELY — no charge
GIVE — it is a gift
US — Christians
ALL — all means all
THINGS — physical blessings

I am sure spiritual blessings are included in the above listing, but the context of the verse certainly implies the blood of Jesus not only provided our salvation in the spiritual realm, but also our material blessings in the physical realm in which we now live on earth.

I see the blood of Jesus in 11 Corinthians 5:21, which is called the heart of the Gospel:

> *[21]For he hath made him to be sin for us, who new no sin; that we might be made the righteousness of God in him.*

God *"made Him to be sin"* at the cross where Jesus' blood was shed. We thereby were *"made the righteousness of God in Him"* at the cross. How do I receive this righteousness? By my faith. Faith in what? Again, the object, the foundation of my faith is the shed blood of Jesus Christ.

Chapter 5

Faith in the Blood

For no one can lay any foundation other than the one already laid, which is Jesus Christ.
—*1 Corinthians 3:11*

> **FOUNDATION:** *that on which something is founded; the basis or groundwork of anything.*

When I place my faith in the blood of Jesus Christ, my faith is founded on what the blood did for me at the cross nearly 2,000 years ago, and what the blood is doing for me right now during my lifetime on earth.

Past Tense

Many Scriptures detailing what the blood purchased for us at the cross were listed in the second chapter. Our benefits of redemption, forgiveness of sins, cleansing, justification, reconciliation, sanctification, peace, approach to

39

God, eternal inheritance, and healing made up that list. And I am sure the list is not complete. The point I am making is that these benefits are past tense in the sense that Jesus died on the cross for us just once (Hebrews 9:12, 28). He will not do it again. God has no other plan to reconcile the human race to Himself. We received these benefits when we became Christians.

Present Tense

The blood of Jesus Christ is also active in our behalf today. The search for the blood as an object for my faith uncovered a most amazing fact: the blood of Christ still speaks today!

> [22]But ye are come unto mount Zion, and unto the city of the living God, the heavenly Jerusalem, and to an innumerable company of angels,
> [23]To the general assembly and church of the firstborn, which are written in heaven, and to God the Judge of all, and to the spirits of just men made perfect,
> [24]And to Jesus the mediator of the new covenant, and to the blood of sprinkling, that speaketh better things than that of Abel.   (Hebrews 12:22-24)

Notice the six living entities in heaven according to this single passage: angels, the redeemed church, God, spirits of the righteous who have reached perfection, Jesus, and the blood that speaks. Everything listed is alive! And in the same list is the blood. The blood of Jesus is alive, and it speaks better things than Abel's blood.

Recall that Abel's blood spoke after he was murdered by his brother Cain:

> *[10]And He [God] said, What hast thou done? the voice of thy brother's blood crieth unto me from the ground.* (Genesis 4:10)

Notice too, that Hebrews 12:24 implies that Abel's blood still speaks today:

> *[24]The blood of sprinkling, the speaketh better things than that of Abel.*

I imagine Abel's blood speaks for revenge, justice, and vengeance. I am sure the blood of Jesus speaks love, forgiveness, grace, and mercy in accordance with His character.

A Foundation for Faith

What a foundation, what a basis for faith! My faith is in the blood of Jesus Christ shed on the cross (past tense) and in the same blood of Jesus Christ that still speaks today (present tense).

Other Scriptures that reveal that the blood of Jesus is living today are Hebrews 10:19-20, 1 Peter 1:2, and 1 John 5:8. For an expansion of this marvelous truth, see the last section of this book.

The blood of Jesus is alive. It speaks of what it has accomplished at the cross. It speaks on our behalf today.

My faith has an object. It is the blood of Jesus Christ. What a solid foundation for faith!

PART TWO:

The Lord's Supper, More Than a Ritual

Chapter 6

More Than A Ritual

RITUAL: *an established or prescribed procedure for a religious or other rite.*

B eaming at me, the overweight middle-aged woman in the blue dress exclaimed, "Thank you so very much. I have never understood that part about the Lord's Supper before."

I just stood there smiling for a moment. "Thank you," I quickly recovered. "It was years before I understood it, too."

In June 1977, a pastor friend had asked my wife and myself to oversee the morning worship service at his church. We agreed and started making plans. My wife would lead the worship and hymn singing. One elder would make the announcements, and another would supervise the offering. I would preach the sermon after the choir sang the last anthem.

"Oh, by the way," added our friend, "would you also minister communion? We do it every Sunday morning in our church."

"I would love to," I responded, glancing at my wife for some kind of confirmation. "This will be a first-time experience for us."

I felt the service went well. The sermon on the subject of healing was short, to the point, and well received. I then called the ushers forward and read 1 Corinthians 11:23-31. I commented briefly on the first four verses and then focused more on the remaining five:

> [27]Wherefore whosoever shall eat this bread, and drink this cup of the Lord, unworthily, shall be guilty of the body and blood of the Lord.
> [28]But let a man examine himself, and so let him eat of that bread, and drink of that cup.
> [29]For he that eateth and drinketh unworthily, eateth and drinketh damnation to himself, not discerning the Lord's body.
> [30]For this cause many are weak and sickly among you, and many sleep.
> [31]For if we would judge ourselves, we should not be judged.
> (1 Corinthians 11:27-31)

I remember telling the congregation that these verses reveal yet another way in which God heals people today. I did this deliberately to help tie the sermon together with what we were about to do in administering the Lord's supper.

Brian Williams, a minister in Birmingham, England, illustrates what I was relating to that congregation. He testifies in his book, *The Holy Communion:*

> The writer remembers one occasion when, during a Crusade in the north of England, he was afflicted with a heat rash that produced a crop of itching spots all over his body. He prayed for healing, claimed the Lord's deliverance, stood upon the healing promises of Christ, and even received the laying-on of hands, all to no avail. Then at the Breaking of Bread service on Sunday morning, believing that there was a provision for healing in the Communion service, he discerned the Lord's healthy body, appropriated the abundant life of Christ, and was healed the same day.
>
> Since that time, we have taught the people in our meetings that they can receive healing in the Communion when they are sick, but more important still, the very reason for Christ's institution of the Sacrament is that we might partake of His eternal life. Divine health is better than Divine healing! (Williams 1964, p. 18)

"In like manner," I admonished the people that Sunday, "examine yourselves. Get right with one another and with God. Then expect Him to heal you as you partake of the elements."

The ushers then took charge of passing the bread and grape juice. After a few closing words, I gave the benediction. Then my wife and I made our way to the church door to greet the people. That is when the woman in the blue dress thanked us and spoke those words that I have often thought about, "I have never understood that part about the Lord's Supper before."

Reflections

Afterwards, in talking about this with our pastor friend, he said that he often used the very same Scriptures as I did. It was probably a case of the woman hearing the Scriptures but not understanding them. She had been a long-time member of that church. Her church ministered communion every Sunday. And yet she never understood one of the fundamental reasons why we take the Lord's Supper.

Why do we take communion? I had no better understanding than the woman in the blue dress for most of my life. I took communion but really didn't understand why. All I got out of it for years and years were the words, *"This do in remembrance of me,"* and *"For as often as you eat this bread, and drink this cup, you do show the Lord's death till he come"* (1 Corinthians 11:24-26).

I had always looked backward in time to the cross by *"remembrance"* and forward in time to the rapture by *"till he come."* I never looked to the **now**, the time in which we live. In fact, it has been only recently that I began to search for a more complete understanding of the Lord's Supper.

Discoveries

The search was indeed very fruitful. I found that the Scriptures reveal that only two ordinances were observed by the early Christians. These were water baptism, a one-time act, and the Lord's Supper. Although both were of very great importance in the early church, this book deals only with the ordinance of the Lord's Supper.

Before the Gospels and Epistles were written, before the conversion of Paul, before the Gospel was preached to the Gentiles, early Christians were celebrating the Lord's Supper. We know this from Acts 2:42 which states:

> *[42]And they continued steadfastly in the apostle's doctrine and fellowship, and in breaking of bread, and in prayers.*

Acts 2:46 confirms this with the statement, *"Breaking bread from house to house."*

This fact is worth emphasizing, for both the preaching of the Gospel and partaking of the Supper has always characterized Christians taking the message of the cross to the ends of the earth.

In searching out a more complete understanding of the Lord's Supper, I discovered three fundamental concepts uttered from the lips of Jesus on this subject. All three are somewhat foreign to our western minds. They are not a part of our culture. Yet, we need to know about them to really understand what Jesus meant when He instituted communion at the Last Supper the night before He was crucified. They are the Passover, the blood covenant, and the kingdom of God.

From reading and meditating on all the Scriptures concerning the Lord's Supper, I found that Jesus assumed that His hearers were familiar with these three concepts. I say this because they didn't question Him about what He was saying to them. Scripture records Jesus' disciples questioned Him about many other things. But it appears that these fundamental concepts were so familiar to them that they did not require further elaboration. However, because of my western culture and background and a separation of some 2,000 years in time, I found that I had to understand the Passover, blood covenant, and kingdom of God before I could have a more accurate understanding of the Lord's Supper.

So, I thank the woman in the blue dress. Her honest statement that she didn't understand everything in taking communion reminded me of my fruitful search for aspects about the Lord's Supper that I had investigated only a few years before. I pray that deeper meaning for the body of Christ of the significance and power found in this commemorative celebration may result from the truths presented here.

Chapter 7

The Passover

PASSOVER: *A Jewish festival, beginning on the eve of the fourteenth day of Nisan and celebrated for either seven or eight days, that commemorates the Exodus. (The Jewish month of Nisan corresponds approximately to our month of April. Also, Jesus was crucified during the annual celebration of the Passover.)*

EXODUS: *the departure of the Israelites from Egypt under Moses; the second book of the Bible, containing an account of the Exodus.*

The moment I read the words *"Christ, our Passover lamb, has been sacrificed"* (1 Corinthians 5:7 NIV), I knew within me that knowledge of the ancient Passover event would help to yield more understanding about the Lord's Supper.

Why did Paul call Christ *"our Passover lamb"*? Why did he refer the Gentile believers at Corinth to an event involving Israelites which took place some 1,500 years earlier? Let us look to the biblical account of the Passover for our answers.

The Exodus

I believe the best Old Testament type of our redemption is found in the Exodus from Egypt. Let us center on the Passover account when some 2,500,000 Israelites were delivered from 430 years of slavery in Egypt under the leadership of Moses by the miracles of God.

The incident is related in the book of Exodus as follows:

> *⁴And Moses said, Thus saith the Lord, about midnight will I go out into the midst of Egypt:*
> *⁵and all the firstborn in the land of Egypt shall die.* (Exodus 11:4-5)

More of the event is unfolded in the twelfth chapter:

> *¹And the Lord spake unto Moses and Aaron in the land of Egypt, saying,*

> [3]...*take to them every man a lamb...a lamb for an house.*
> [6]*And the whole assembly of the congregation of Israel shall kill it in the evening.*
> [7]*And they shall take of the blood, and strike it on the two side posts and on the upper door post of the houses, wherein they shall eat it.*
> [13]*And the blood shall be to you for a token* [sign] *upon the houses where ye are: and when I see the blood, I will pass over you, and the plague shall not be upon you to destroy you, when I smite the land of Egypt.* (Exodus 12:1,3,6,7,13)

Continue to read the account in Exodus 12:21-23 where Moses told the elders of Israel what the Lord had told him. Note the words *"the Lord will pass over the door"* in verse 23. If the blood was not applied, death surely came:

> [30]*And Pharaoh rose up in the night, he, and all his servants, and all the Egyptians; and there was a great cry in Egypt, for there was not a house where there was not one dead.* (Exodus 12:30)

During that momentous night in Egypt, the Israelites were spared the death of their firstborn by following God's instructions given through Moses. This tenth and final plague did not come upon the Israelites. This miraculous event is known as the Passover.

Let us get the definition of the Passover straight from the Bible. In Exodus 12:26-27, we read:

> [26]*And it shall come to pass, when your children shall say unto you, What mean ye by this service?*
> [27]*That ye shall say, It is the sacrifice of the Lord's passover, who passed over the houses of the children of Israel in Egypt, when he smote the Egyptians, and delivered our houses.*

The blood of the sacrificed lamb applied to the lintel and door posts was the sign for judgment to spare the Israelites' firstborn from death.

But have you ever noticed what happened to the body of the sacrificed lamb?

> [8]*And they shall eat the flesh in that night, roast with fire*
> [9]*...his head with his legs, and with the purtenance thereof.*
> [11]*And thus shall ye eat it; with your loins girded, your shoes on your feet, and your staff in your hand, and ye shall eat it in haste: it is the Lord's passover.*
>
> (Exodus 12:8-9,11)

The Blood and the Body

The blood was to be applied, the body was to be eaten. For the Israelites, the blood of the Passover lamb saved them, and the body of the Passover lamb healed them. For we read in another Scripture,

> [37]*He brought them forth also with silver and gold, and there was not one feeble person among their tribes. (Psalm 105:37)*

It is obvious to me that a people in slavery for 430 years would be weak, infirm, diseased. Certainly I would assume there were those who were on stretchers or used crutches or were sick. But as the miracle of the blood on the doorposts delivered their firstborn from death, another miracle was simultaneously happening. The Israelites were all healed while eating the Passover lamb. This was undoubtedly the greatest mass miracle service that has ever happened. God miraculously prepared His people to travel *"by day and night"* for several days without exhaustion (Exodus 13:17-22). We are talking about approximately 2.5 million Israelites and yet *"there was not one feeble person among their tribes."*

The blood and the body! Jesus' death for our life! The blood of *"Christ, our Passover lamb"* (1 Corinthians 5:7 NIV) has saved us.

The body of *"Christ, our Passover lamb"* bore stripes for our physical healing. The blood and body of Jesus has provided our salvation and our healing.

Faith in the Blood

Let us put ourselves in the shoes of an Israelite slave in Egypt for a moment. Imagine the following situation. One afternoon there is a loud rap at the door. Upon opening it, the slave sees his neighborhood councilman anxiously standing before him.

"Yes, what is it?" questions the slave.

"I have just been commanded by my superior to tell everyone in our neighborhood the most amazing instructions," blurts out the nervous councilman.

"Commanded? Instructions? What about?"

"Quick! You are to kill your best one-year-old unblemished male lamb. Sprinkle its blood around the frame of your front door. Then barbecue the carcass for supper. In particular, you must eat all of it including the entrails," the councilman rapidly orders.

"Why? What is happening?" the slave rightfully questions.

"These instructions have come down through the chain of command from Moses," the messenger shouts as he hurries towards the next house. "Moses said the tenth and final plague would cover Egypt tonight. If you fail to follow these instructions, something terrible will happen."

"Wait! What will happen?" the slave shouts back.

The answer stuns the slave. "Your first-born child will die!"

Our Turn

How many of us would have acted on these instructions, carrying them out completely?

Let us reflect for a moment on this situation from Exodus 12. If we take the round number of ten persons per family to eat their Passover lamb, approximately 250,000 lambs were being roasted on the same night. The Egyptian task masters must have known that something was up! The Israelites, never doubting God would deliver them, did all they were told to do by faith in **verbal** instructions.

In the same way today, we have instructions given in the written Word of God concerning the Lord's Supper *"Christ, our Passover lamb"* speaks to us, His disciples, *"Take, eat: this is my body, which is broken for you: do this in remembrance of me"* (1 Corinthians 11:24). His body was broken for us that we may be healed. *"By his stripes ye were healed"* (1 Peter

2:24). In addition, *"Christ, our Passover lamb"* says to His church, *"Drink ye all of it; for this is my blood of the new testament, which is shed for many for the remission of sins"* (Matthew 26:27-28). His blood was shed for the remission of sins, our redemption. *"In whom we have redemption through his blood, the forgiveness of sins"* (Ephesians 1:7).

What do we as Christians do with these **written** instructions? Compared with the verbal instructions given to the Israelite slave, they really are not difficult at all. He was to actually kill a lamb, sprinkle its blood over the door frame of his house, and then proceed to eat all of it. That included its head and entrails. He did this by faith in the verbal instructions he received.

On the other hand, all we are required to do is to take emblems of the body and blood of *"Christ, our Passover lamb"* and appropriate them by faith for the remission of our sins and for the healing of our bodies.

Healing Today

I imagine the woman in the blue dress patiently hearing this explanation of how the Passover relates to the Lord's Supper through *"Christ, our Passover lamb."* I can further anticipate her question at this point. It would undoubtedly be something like, "What I don't fully understand is how you can say the broken body of Jesus is for our healing today."

I would try to answer her question by asking her one, "When were you saved by the blood of Jesus?"

She would probably answer, "Well, when I was twelve years old, I accepted Christ as my Savior."

I would gently say, "Sister, your salvation was paid for almost 2,000 years ago. You received it for yourself when you were twelve."

Then I would ask, "When was your healing provided?"

After a moment's reflection, she would light up and exclaim, "Well, 2,000 years ago, also! Jesus is not going to heal us—He already has. We receive it now when we need it."

I would show her in the Bible why we may expect healing when we take communion. Remember, Paul wrote the Corinthians what he *"received from the Lord"* (1 Corinthians 11:23). What did the Lord tell him about healing and health? The key verse is:

[30]*For this cause many are weak and sickly among you, and many sleep.*
                                    (1 Corinthians 11:30)

From this, it is plain that many Christians among the Corinthians were weak and sick and many had already died.

Let us look *"for this cause"* for the sorry state of health among this early church. Reading over 1 Corinthians 11:17-21, we find that when the Corinthians met together to observe the Lord's Supper, ungodly things were taking place. There were divisions and heresies. Some persons were rude and rushed to eat their own supper while other church members remained hungry. Still other Corinthians were drunk. Paul then scolds them and tells them again what the Lord Jesus Christ had revealed to him concerning the very words and actions of that first Lord's Supper.

Verses 27-29 contain the warning with the key word *"unworthily"* used twice. What is meant by taking the Lord's Supper *"unworthily"*? Listed again: divisions, heresies, gluttony, selfishness, drunkenness. The result? *"For this cause many are weak and sickly among you, and many sleep."*

Then I would ask the woman, "Taken in context, what do the five words *'not discerning the Lord's body'* of verse 29 have to do with weakness, sickness, and death of verse 30?"

I can imagine her stumbling over the words *"not discerning."* Reaching for a dictionary, I would offer her some help.

DISCERN: *recognize as distinct or different; discriminate.*

"Well," she would reason, "to not discern the Lord's body would be to not recognize the Lord's body as distinct or different." I would let her think for a moment. "In other words," she would continue, "when Jesus said, *'Take, eat, this is my body which is broken for you,'* I have to discern something, wouldn't I?"

"Go on," I would smile.

"Let me get this straight," she would think out loud. "If I eat and drink the Lord's Supper in an unworthy manner and do not discern the Lord's body, then I may expect weakness, sickness, and death to be the result. Conversely, if I take the Lord's Supper in a worthy manner and discern the Lord's body, then I may expect just the opposite of weakness, sickness, and death."

"Give me the punch line," I would tease.

"I see it!" she would exclaim. "Just as Jesus' blood was shed to forgive our sins, Jesus' body was bruised to provide for our physical healing. That is, Jesus also died for my sicknesses and diseases. If I discern His broken body as able to provide healing, then when I take communion, I may expect strength, healing, and therefore a long, healthy life!"

"That's right! You've got it!" I would rejoice with her.

"Thank God I am beginning to understand the Lord's Supper," she would smile.

"Good. Did you notice 1 Corinthians 11:29 says *'not discerning the Lord's body'* instead of saying *'not discerning the Lord's blood'*? Since Paul was writing to Christians, they undoubtedly discerned Jesus' blood for their salvation. But the weakness, sickness, and death of verse 30 was the price they were paying for not discerning the Lord's body for their healing.

"In the J.B. Phillips version, verse 30 reads very forcefully as: *'It is this careless participation which is the reason for the many feeble and sickly Christians in your church.'* Correctly discerning Jesus' body is necessary for healing.

"And one last thing," I would add. "The Passover is a Jewish observance today. They celebrate the Exodus from slavery in Egypt. The blood of the lamb saved the firstborn from destruction, and the body of the lamb healed them because *'there was not one feeble person among the tribes'* (Psalms 105:37).

"In a similar manner, the Lord's Supper is a Christian observance today. We celebrate our exodus from *'the power of darkness'* and our translation *'into the kingdom of his dear Son'* (Colossians 1:13). The blood of *'Christ, our Passover lamb'* has saved us from *'perishing'* (John 3:16), and the body of *'Christ, our*

Passover lamb' provides our health and healing (1 Peter 2:24)."

Then and Now

With a twinkle in my eye I would add, "Do you know that the Bible plainly says our Lord Jesus Christ ministered to the Israelites in the Exodus some 1,450 years before He walked on this planet as a man?"

"No," she would gasp. "Where does it say that?"

I would say, "Read 1 Corinthians 10:3-4 where it says: *'And did all eat the same spiritual meat, and did all drink the same spiritual drink: for they drank of that spiritual Rock that followed them: and that Rock was Christ.'*"

"Well," she would respond, "If Christ ministered to them with spiritual food and drink some 1,450 years **before** He was born, it is easy for me to believe that He ministers to us with spiritual food and drink in the communion service some 1,950 years **after** He was resurrected!"

Amen! It would be hard to improve on a conclusion like that.

Chapter 8

The Blood Covenant

BLOOD: *the fluid that circulates in the principal vascular system of man and other vertebrates; the vital principle, life.*

BLOOD BROTHER: *a person's brother by birth; a male person bound to another by ties of great friendship; a male bound to another male by a specific ritual, usually the commingling of blood.*

COVENANT: *an agreement, usually formal, between two or more persons to do or not do something specified; the conditional promises made to man by God, as revealed in the Scripture.*

T he various accounts of the Lord's Supper found in Scripture all include a reference to the blood of Jesus linked with a new covenant. An example is *"This cup is the new testament in my blood"* (1 Corinthians 11:25). Since testament and covenant are translated from the same Greek word, this verse could read, *"This cup is the new covenant in my blood"* as in the New International Version. A complete understanding of the Lord's Supper, therefore, requires a comprehension of covenants made with blood.

Some Background

A covenant, or agreement, or contract, ratified by the shedding of blood, is not common in our culture. It has little meaning to our western mind. However, H. Clay Trumbull in his classic book, *The Blood Covenant,* states:

> From the beginning, and everywhere, blood seems to have been looked upon as pre-eminently the representative of life; as, indeed, in peculiar sense, life itself. The transference of blood from one organism to another has been counted the transference of life, with all that life includes. The inter-commingling of blood by its inter-transference has been understood as equivalent to an inter-commingling of natures. Two natures thus inter-commingled, by the inter-commingling of blood, have been considered as forming, thence forward, one blood, one life, one nature, one soul—in two organisms...
>
> The mode of inter-transference of blood, with all that this carries, has been deemed

practicable, alike by way of the lips and by way of the opened and inter-flowing veins. It has also been represented by blood-bathing, by blood-anointing, and by blood-sprinkling; or, again, by the inter-drinking of wine—which was formerly commingled with blood itself in the drinking...

A covenant of blood, a covenant made by the inter-commingling of blood, has been recognized as the closest, the holiest, and the most indissoluble, compact conceivable. Such a covenant clearly involves an absolute surrender of one's separate self, and an irrevocable merging of one's individual nature into the dual, or the multiplied, personality included in the compact. Man's highest and noblest out-reachings of soul have, therefore, been for such a union with the divine nature as is typified in this human covenant of blood....

Proofs of the existence of this rite of blood-covenanting have been found among primitive peoples of all quarters of the globe; and its antiquity is carried back to a date long prior to the days of Abraham.

(Trumbull 1975, pp. 202-206)

Perhaps an example from Trumbull's book will illustrate the concept of a blood covenant:

Another of the methods by which the rite of blood-friendship was observed in the Norseland, was by causing the blood of the two covenanting persons to inter-flow from their pierced hands, while they lay together underneath a lifted sod. The idea involved seems to have been, the burial of the two individuals, in

their separate personal lives, and the intermingling of those lives—by the intermingling of
their blood—while in their temporary grave; in
order to their rising again with a common
life—one life, one soul, in two bodies.

(Trumbull 1975, pp. 41-42)

A Personal Example

A personal example, taken from the day in
which we live, will help to confirm Trumbull's
statements. Our family served a three-year
missionary term in Zimbabwe in southern
Africa from 1973 to 1976. During that time I
remember asking a black friend about the
practice of the blood covenant in his country.
He responded that indeed such covenants still
take place but only in rare instances.

However, he then went on to describe an
alternative practice in widespread use today in
Zimbabwe. The way I interpreted what he
explained was that the practice has the same
deep meaning of a blood covenant but without
the gory ritual of shedding each others' blood.

My friend explained that whatever was
owned by one party automatically belonged to
the other party. As an example, I remember his
telling me that as we were there in his home
talking, his covenant friend could arrive, get in
my friend's car parked in the driveway, and
drive off. No permission would have to be

given, no question asked. By having entered into such a covenant, my friend's car (and anything else) belonged to his covenant partner. And my friend had the same reciprocal rights with his covenant partner.

God's Covenants

This concept, applied to the covenants established between God and man, is so tremendous that it is almost unbelievable. Simply stated, the new covenant (the New Testament) means **whatever God has belongs to us, and whatever we have belongs to Him.** Numerous Scriptures actually exhibit this relationship between God and man. Two of my favorites are in Romans:

> [16]*The Spirit itself beareth witness with our spirit, that we are the children of God,* [17]*and if children, then heirs of God, and joint-heirs with Christ. (Romans 8:16-17)*

> [32]*He that spared not his own Son, but delivered him up for us all, how shall he not with him also freely give us all things? (Romans 8:32)*

In other words, as Christians, we are *"heirs of God,"* and God will *"freely give us all things!"*

With this introduction, I am sure the woman in the blue dress would naturally want to know what the blood covenant has to do with the Lord's Supper. I would begin my explanation by recalling several verses where it is explicitly mentioned:

> [27]*Drink ye all of it;*
> [28]*For this is my blood of the new test-ament.* *(Matthew 26:27-28)*

> [20]*This cup is the new testament in my blood, which is shed for you.* *(Luke 22:20)*

> [25]*This cup is the new covenant in my blood.* *(1 Corinthians 11:25 NIV)*

Again, the concept of linking blood to a covenant (testament) is not known in our culture. So I would then try to help my friend with an example from the old covenant (testament) before explaining the basis of the new covenant (testament).

David and Jonathan

In 1 Samuel 17, we read the familiar story of David and Goliath. But have you ever read what happened after David told King Saul about the encounter?

¹The soul of Jonathan [King Saul's son]
was knit with the soul of David, and Jona-
than loved him as his own soul.
³Then Jonathan and David made a cove-
nant, because he loved him as his own
soul. *(1 Samuel 18:1,3)*

⁴Jonathan swore to be his blood brother,
and sealed the pact by giving him his robe,
sword, bow, and belt. (1 Samuel 18:4 TLB)

One translation says *"covenant,"* and the
other says *"blood brother."* I put the two together and conclude that David and Jonathan
made a blood covenant. A reading of Trumbull's
book leaves little doubt about the universal
common practice of blood covenants between
men. However, the law states, *"Ye shall not cut*
yourselves" (Deuteronomy 14:1). Consequently,
I believe David and Jonathan made a blood
covenant without the commingling of their
blood. In any case, the covenant they made was
very strong as we shall see.

Notice that Jonathan sealed the covenant
by giving David his garments and sword. This
represented that whatever belonged to Jonathan now belonged to David. David, a shepherd
boy at that time, could not reciprocate with
such wealth of fine clothing and weapons. But
it didn't matter in their covenant.

Notice, also, a more amazing fact. That is,
Jonathan, as the king's son, was to be the next

king of Israel. A prince and a shepherd boy made a covenant! We do know that God had anointed David to be the next king. But in a covenant relationship, that fact didn't matter either. *"The soul of Jonathan was knit with the soul of David, and Jonathan loved him as his own soul"* (1 Samuel 18:1).

Later, the Bible again states:

> *[16]So Jonathan made a covenant with the house of David...*
> *[17]And Jonathan caused David to swear again, because he loved him: for he loved him as he loved his own soul.*
> *(1 Samuel 20:16-17)*

Again, in the same chapter and in stronger language, we read:

> *[42]And Jonathan said to David, Go in peace, for as much as we have sworn both of us in the name of the Lord, saying, The Lord be between me and thee, and between my seed and thy seed for ever.*
> *(1 Samuel 20:42)*

This is important because of the words *"for ever."* Notice how David promised King Saul he would, in effect, honor the covenant he had made with Jonathan. That is, Saul's children and Jonathan's children and their descendants would be in a covenant relationship with David

and David's children *"forever."* (See 1 Samuel
24:21-22.)

Mephibosheth

The story continues after King Saul and
Jonathan were killed by the Philistines. (See 1
Samuel 31.) Jonathan had a son named Mephibosheth, who was only five years old when his
father and grandfather were killed. In the
panic to flee the palace into hiding for fear of a
purge of the house of Saul, Mephibosheth was
injured and became lame in both feet (11
Samuel 4:4).

I imagine that Mephibosheth, actually next
in line by natural succession to be king, was
raised in the wilderness in poverty, fear, and
hatred of David, God's choice for the next king.
Mephibosheth's life was tragic—he really was
in a blood covenant relationship with King
David through his father, Jonathan. But,
apparently, he didn't know it. Yet, the terms of
the covenant included him and, indeed, his
seed *"forever."*

The brief account of 11 Samuel 9 reveals
the power and the benefits of a blood covenant.
We read in the first verse how King David
recalled the covenant he had made with *"the
house of Saul."* He wanted to honor it *"for
Jonathan's sake."* A drama began when David

called for Jonathan's son, Mephibosheth (11 Samuel 9:1-5).

Can you imagine the fear and terror that Mephibosheth experienced when the king's soldiers searched him out and brought him before David? We see in verse six, *"He fell on his face, and did reverence."* David calmed him in verse seven by saying, *"Fear not."* And in verse eight, Mephibosheth calls himself *"a dead dog."* Again, Mephibosheth was in a blood covenant relationship with King David, but he didn't know it!

Because of the covenant with Jonathan and his seed *"forever,"* David gave to Mephibosheth all the land of Saul, residence in the palace, and servants to wait upon him. Note that David calls Mephibosheth *"as one of the king's sons"* (verse 11).

Wasn't the covenant powerful? Mephibosheth called himself *"a dead dog,"* but David considered him *"as one of the king's sons."*

Consider what **could have** happened at this point. Mephibosheth could have said, "This is a trick. I don't believe it. If I ever get out of here alive, I'm going back to the desert to live." Even after finding out that his father, Jonathan, had made a covenant with David, Mephibosheth could have refused it and returned to his old life.

Consider also what **did** happen. Mephibosheth had to die to his former life and enter into the provisions of the covenant. He had to accept what was offered as a free gift. He didn't deserve to be as David's own son, but he chose to accept it. He had to radically change his life style from poverty in the desert to riches in the king's palace.

I want to stress a very important point that will surface later in discussing the covenant in relationship to the Lord's Supper. Any king could elevate any peasant from rags to riches, so to speak. The peasant would point to the king's benevolence as the reason he was chosen. But, note the fact that the opposite could happen. That is, any day the king could strip the peasant of his riches and privileges and send him back whence he came, but not so under a covenant relationship. Mephibosheth had the **right** to his inheritance. He belonged at the king's table. Even though Mephibosheth would undoubtedly be the first to admit that he didn't deserve it, he would say he had the right to be treated as if he were his father Jonathan. Mephibosheth had the right to be elevated from rags to riches because of the blood covenant. In fact, the covenant was entered into before he was born.

Said another way, the covenant that Mephibosheth was under would never be broken. It was *"forever."* Mephibosheth never had to consider that he would be ousted from

David's palace and sent back to scratch out an existence in the desert.

We, too, need to understand the power and provisions of a blood covenant.

A New Covenant for Us

I would pause at this point and watch the effect of this covenant example sweep over the woman in the blue dress. Her first reaction would probably be enjoyment of the story I have just related. Also, she would acknowledge that the idea of a blood covenant is indeed foreign to her. Undoubtedly, she would see how far-reaching it is, especially that it includes those unborn at the time the covenant was made.

After she would talk it over for a moment, I would remind her that the words *"covenant"* and *"testament"* are translated from the same Greek word in the Bible. Then the obvious thought would be expressed, "What does the New Testament or new covenant mean to us today? Is it a blood covenant? Am I like Mephibosheth?" Her eyes would open wider. "Am I under a blood covenant and don't know it?" she would exclaim, thinking about the power and provisions of such a relationship.

"Okay, okay," I would interrupt, holding up my hand. "As Christians, we **are** under a blood

78

covenant. It is called the new covenant or the New Testament. We are a covenant people whether we **know** it or not. And if we know it, we are still a covenant people whether we **believe** it or not. Let my try to explain the exciting fact that as Mephibosheth was in Jonathan, so are we in Jesus Christ."

The very foundation of my explanation would be the fact that God has entered into a blood covenant with the human race. He has done this through Jesus Christ. He has done it because He loves us. The covenant exists whether we know about it or not. It exists whether we believe it or not. This covenant is everlasting. And we can enter into this covenant relationship with God through Jesus Christ.

An Analogy

Let my illustrate with an analogy. Let King David represent God. Let Jonathan represent Jesus Christ. Let Mephibosheth represent us. As David and Jonathan made a blood covenant that included Mephibosheth, so God the Father and God the Son made a blood covenant that includes us. As Mephibosheth lived in fear, ignorance, and poverty until he learned he was *as one of the king's sons,* so we live in fear, ignorance, and poverty until we learn we are in a covenant relationship with God.

Again, as Mephibosheth experienced the power and provisions of his covenant with David only through his father Jonathan, we enter into the new covenant with God only through our Lord and Savior Jesus Christ. Mephibosheth was born after his covenant was made. We were born after our covenant was established. Mephibosheth entered into his covenant relationship by believing the words that King David told him. We enter into our covenant relationship by believing the words of the new covenant (testament).

Establishment of Our Covenant

What are some Scriptures that tell us we are in a covenant relationship with God through Jesus Christ? There are many. Two that I shared earlier are in Romans, chapter 8. They bear repetition:

> *16The Spirit itself beareth witness with our spirit, that we are the children of God:*
> *17And if children, then heirs, heirs of God, and joint-heirs with Christ.*
> *(Romans 8:16-17)*

*[32]He that spared not his own Son, but
delivered him up for us all, how shall he
not with him also freely give us all things?
(Romans 8:32)*

Note these Scriptures mention God, Jesus,
the Holy Spirit and us. We cannot enter into a
blood covenant relationship with God by ourselves. Our covenant relationship with God
must come through Jesus Christ. As He so
clearly said, *"No man cometh unto the Father,
but by me"* (John 14:6). We can't do it, but
praise God, Jesus already has!

And how was the new covenant established
through Jesus? It came from the fact that
Jesus was born as God incarnate—100 percent
God and 100 percent man. God, in a human
body named Jesus, really walked and lived on
planet earth. I believe it is true that Jesus was
God's representative on earth as 100 percent
God, and, at the same time, He was also man's
representative as 100 percent man. That is,
when Jesus' blood was shed at the cruel whipping post and on the cross, a blood covenant
was established between God and man—both
through the God-Man Jesus Christ. **God entered into covenant with man through the
blood of Jesus, and man entered into
covenant with God through that same
blood.** Pure, innocent blood was shed to ratify
a new covenant that can never be broken.

Now, we as Christians are reconciled to God through Jesus (11 Corinthians 5:18) as Mephibosheth was reconciled to David through Jonathan. Even though Mephibosheth belonged to *the house of Saul* by natural birth, he became *as one of the king's sons* by virtue of a blood covenant.

Likewise, even though we belonged to the world, to *the power of darkness* by natural birth, we became *sons of God* by virtue of the new covenant established through the blood of Jesus.

For the sake of completeness, but also keeping in mind that I may be stretching the analogy too far, I believe those 36 servants (11 Samuel 9:10-12) ministering the things of David's kingdom to Mephibosheth correspond to the Holy Spirit ministering the things of the kingdom of God to us. I further believe that those servants also represent angels, *sent forth to minister for them who shall be heirs of salvation* (Hebrews 1:1).

The very reason God took the initiative and sent Jesus into this world to establish a covenant by His blood was for the reconciliation of man (11 Corinthians 5:18). Our part is to respond to such love. Our part is to accept what God has provided. Like Mephibosheth before David, we can accept or reject the provisions of the covenant. We can move into the king's palace, so to speak, or we can continue to live in the desert. We have a choice. We can choose life or death.

Let us accept what God has provided. As Mephibosheth could approach King David's throne after he realized he was *"as one of the king's sons," "let us therefore come boldly unto the throne of grace"* (Hebrews 4:16) of Almighty God. What a call for fellowship with God! What an invitation to take our needs to Him! What a blessing to know that God will *"also freely give us all things"* (Romans 8:32) because we are partakers of the new covenant.

Old Things Have Passed Away

Again I would pause and let my friend consider all these things I was saying. "Does this make any sense to you?" I would probe.

"I must feel like Mephibosheth when he was brought before the King," she would ponder. "It is a feeling of 'can this really be true?' mixed with a feeling of unworthiness."

"I know it. I've experienced the same thing," I would reassure her.

"Can you summarize what you have been telling me?" she would ask.

"I will try," I would say as several conclusions would come to mind.

"First, our approach to God is not based on what we have or haven't done. Our approach is based on the finished work of the blood covenant established by Jesus Christ. This covenant exists whether we know it or not.

"Second, once we know such a covenant exists, we must accept and believe it. Hebrews 11:6 sums up the matter: *'But without faith it is impossible to please him. For he that cometh to God must believe that he is, and that he is a rewarder of them that diligently seek him.'*

"Paraphrasing this verse we could say: *'For he that cometh to God must believe that he is [a **blood-covenant-making God**], and that He is a rewarder [a **blood-covenant-keeping God**] of them that diligently seek Him.'* God has made and will keep the new covenant. We must know and believe such a blood covenant is ours.

"Third, if God has provided *'all things'* for us, then we will want to reciprocate. We will want to give Him everything we have. And that means **everything,** including our bodies."

> ¹⁹*What? know ye not that your body is the temple of the Holy Ghost which is in you, which ye have of God, and ye are not your own?*
> ²⁰*For ye are bought with a price: therefore glorify God in your body, and in your spirit, which are God's.*
>   (1 Corinthians 6:19-20)

Attitudes

These points speak of a fundamental change of attitude towards God. Consider the Scripture,

> [17]If any man be in Christ, he is a new creature: old things are passed away; behold, all things are become new.
>
> (11 Corinthians 5:17)

Old things, old ways, old attitudes pass away when we realize what the new covenant means. Indeed, *"all things are become new."*

I can imagine Mephibosheth expressed himself along these same lines when he was eating his first meal at the king's table while being waited on by servants assigned to him. Listen to him exclaim, "A few hours ago I considered myself *'as a dead dog.'* Now I am *'as one of the king's sons.'"* Indeed, Mephibosheth, *"old things are passed away; behold, all things are become new."*

What caused such a change in attitude in Mephibosheth? He discovered he was the benefactor of a blood covenant!

What should cause a similar change in attitude in us? The discovery that we are the benefactors of an even better blood covenant!

Jesus associated His blood with a new covenant in the Last Supper discourse. Now we begin to understand the depth and power of His words, *"This cup is the new covenant in my blood"* (1 Corinthians 11:25). Moffat translates Jesus saying, *"This cup means the new covenant ratified by my blood."* The Living Bible expands this as, *"This cup is the new agreement between God and you that has been established and set in motion by my blood."*

As Christians, we have entered into a blood covenant with God through Jesus Christ. Watchman Nee made a profound statement concerning our position and rights under the blood covenant in his book, *The Better Covenant*:

> We do not comprehend the value of the blood; even so, we do not need to evaluate it according to our judgment. We only need to ask God to treat us in accordance with the value of the blood in His sight and the covenant which is sealed by that blood.   (Nee 1982, p. 54)

Chapter 9

The Kingdom of God

KINGDOM: *a state or government having a king or queen as its head; the spiritual sovereignty of God or Christ; the domain over which this extends, whether in heaven or on earth.*

GOD: *the Supreme Being, the creator and ruler of the universe.*

The third concept that needs to be understood for a better appreciation of the Lord's Supper is the New Testament (new covenant) truth of the kingdom of God. The Gospels of Matthew, Mark, and Luke record Jesus making reference to the kingdom of God during His institution of the Lord's Supper.

Why should the kingdom of God be mentioned in these three accounts in relationship to the Lord's Supper? I can imagine my friend in blue asking the same question. I further imagine that even though the explanations of the Passover and the blood covenant were quite enough to satisfy her with a much deeper appreciation of the Lord's Supper, she would also want to consider the marvelous truth of the kingdom of God. She may be sorry (not really!) she ever said, "I have never understood that part about the Lord's Supper before."

Let us begin this part of the search by listing the relevant verses containing reference to the kingdom of God in relation to the Lord's Supper.

> ²⁶*And as they were eating, Jesus took bread, and blessed it, and brake it, and gave it to the disciples, and said, Take, eat; this is my body.*
> ²⁷*And he took the cup, and gave thanks, and gave it to them, saying, Drink ye all of it,*
> *28 For this is my blood of the new testament, which is shed for many for the remission of sins.*
> ²⁹*But I say unto you, I will not drink henceforth of this fruit of the vine, until that day when I drink it new with you in my Father's kingdom.*
>
> *(Matthew 26:26-29)*

> ²⁵*Verily I say unto you, I will drink no more of the fruit of the vine, until that day that I drink it new in the kingdom of God.*
> *(Mark 14:25)*

[18]For I say unto you, I will not drink of the fruit of the vine, until the kingdom of God shall come.   *(Luke 22:18)*

There are so many references to the kingdom of God in the New Testament (but not one in the Old Testament!) that it would take another book to develop this concept more completely. Let me list in summary form some of the main principles of the kingdom of God. Then we will apply these to the Lord's Supper discourse.

What Is the Kingdom of God?

How could I explain the kingdom of God to my friend? I would begin by shortening the dictionary definition at the beginning of this chapter to be simply, "The kingdom of God is God's active reign in heaven and on earth." Then I would need to add Jesus' statement, *"Except a man be born again, he cannot see the kingdom of God"* (John 3:3). Combining these two ideas, we see that God's reign on earth expands as more and more people are born again into His kingdom.

I like the analogy of light representing the kingdom of God. I think of many people standing together in a dark room. One has a lighted candle. He lights the candle of the person next to him. They both light the candle of two other persons. Then the four candles are used to light four others and so on until the room is full of light.

Therefore, I feel a most vivid picture of an expanding kingdom of God is described as:

> [12]*The Father has made us meet* [fit] *to be partakers of the inheritance of the saints in light:*
> [13]*Who has delivered us from the power of darkness, and has translated us into the kingdom of his dear Son:*
> [14]*In whom we have redemption through his blood, even the forgiveness of sins.*
> *(Colossians 1:12-14)*

When we are born again, we change kings, and we also change kingdoms. We are delivered from Satan's kingdom of darkness and translated into the kingdom of God. Light has replaced darkness within us. *"Sons of God"* (Romans 8:14) have replaced those *"having no hope, and without God in the world"* (Ephesians 2:12).

Also, when we change kingdoms, we operate under different laws. It is comparable to our stay in Zimbabwe. During that three year period, we lived under a set of laws different from those of the United States. It is the same way in the spiritual realm. Before we became Christians, we operated under the *"law of sin and death"* (Romans 8:2). Now, as Christians, we operate by spiritual laws that govern God's kingdom such as:

> *²For the law of the Spirit of life in Christ Jesus has made me free from the law of sin and death.*
> *⁵For they that are after the flesh do mind the things of the flesh; but they that are after the Spirit the things of the Spirit.*
> *⁶For to be carnally minded is death; but to be spiritually minded is life and peace.*
> *(Romans 8:2,5,6)*

In fact, much of the eighth chapter of Romans compares these two kingdoms.

Therefore, the kingdom of God is God's rule in human hearts on earth. This kingdom is governed by its spiritual laws. As Christians are *"led by the Spirit of God, they are the sons of God"* (Romans 8:14) helping God to work out His plans and purposes on earth.

God's Will

The Lord's prayer is perhaps the best definition of the kingdom of God. As you know, it begins:

> *⁹Our Father which art in heaven, Hallowed be thy name.*

10Thy kingdom come. Thy will be done in earth, as it is in heaven.

(Matthew 6:9-10)

"Thy kingdom come. Thy will be done in earth" equates the **coming** of God's kingdom with the **doing** of His will. Look at the Scripture again. It begins in heaven and progresses to earth. The link between heaven and earth is *"Thy kingdom come; Thy will be done."* What good would it do for God's kingdom to come to earth if His will isn't done? And, conversely, how can His will be done if His kingdom isn't present? Each part requires the other.

We, born again into the kingdom of God, are to do God's will. In fact, we were created and saved for the purpose of doing His will:

8For by grace are ye saved through faith... 10created in Christ Jesus unto good works, which God hath before ordained that we should walk in them. (Ephesians 2:8,10)

21[God] make you perfect in every good work to do His will. (Hebrews 13:21)

Doing God's will certainly includes preaching the Gospel. I like the last verse of Mark because it shows we are not acting alone in doing God's will:

> [20]*And they went forth, and preached everywhere, the Lord working with them, and confirming the word with signs following.*
>
> (Mark 16:20)

Notice two results of doing God's will: the Lord Jesus is personally present to work with those doing God's will, and He will confirm His Word with signs following.

Application to the Lord's Supper

It is these last two points that I would attempt to expand for the woman whose question prompted all this expounding. I would anticipate her question being something like, "What does the kingdom of God have to do with the Lord's Supper?"

I would answer along these lines: as citizens in the kingdom of God, **when we are doing God's will,** Jesus is personally present, and spiritual laws are at work with signs following.

We need to consider God's will concerning the Lord's Supper. We know His Word expresses His will:

> [23]*For I have received of the Lord that which also I delivered unto you, That the*

Lord Jesus the same night in which he was betrayed took bread:

[24] And when he had given thanks, he brake it, and said, Take, eat; this is my body, which is broken for you: do this in remembrance of me.

[25] After the same manner also he took the cup when he had supped, saying, This cup is the new testament in my blood: this do ye, as oft as ye drink it, in remembrance of me.

[26] For as often as ye eat this bread, and drink this cup, ye show the Lord's death till he come.   (1 Corinthians 11:23-26)

The words *"Do this in remembrance of me"* and *"as often as you eat this bread and drink this cup"* are clear statements of God's will that we are to **regularly** partake of the Lord's Supper. In fact, even before Paul was converted and wrote the above instructions to the church at Cornith, the early Christians were regularly practicing the Lord's Supper as much as they practiced prayer. For we read in Scripture that as early as the Day of Pentecost:

[42] And they continued steadfastly in the apostles' doctrine and fellowship, and in breaking of bread, and in prayers.

(Acts 2:42)

In addition, verse 46 implies the Lord's Supper was practiced daily among the earliest believers:

> *⁴⁶And they, continuing daily with one accord in the temple, and breaking bread from house to house, did eat their meat with gladness and singleness of heart.*
> *(Acts 2:46)*

It is evident that the Lord's Supper was regularly and widely practiced among the early Christians. This is God's will for all believers today because we belong to the same church as the early Christians. Jesus Christ is still the Head of the church. God is still on His throne. Therefore, we need to obey God's will and regularly partake of the bread and the cup. Submission to God's rule is in our very best interests.

Now, with this background, I would attempt to explain to my friend the benefits of obeying God in the matter of regularly partaking of the Lord's Supper.

Personally Present

First of all, Jesus Christ is personally present around His communion table. I base this marvelous fact on three Scriptures.

The first is again Mark 16:20 where the Lord personally worked with those doing God's will as expressed in the Great Commission. The spiritual principle is simply stated: Do God's will, and Jesus will work with you in carrying out that will. It is God's will that we observe the Lord's Supper. Therefore, by doing so in a worthy manner, we may rightfully expect the Lord Jesus to work with us and thereby be personally present.

Notice the same pattern outlined in the Great Commission given at the end of Matthew. The resurrected Christ appeared to His disciples and told them God's will and that He would work with them in carrying out that will:

> ^{19}*Go ye therefore, and teach all nations, baptizing them in the name of the Father, and of the Son, and of the Holy Ghost:*
> ^{20}*Teaching them to observe all things whatsoever I have commanded you. And, lo, I am with you always, even unto the end of the world.*
>
> *(Matthew 28:19-20)*

The second Scripture is found in Paul's first letter to the Corinthians:

> ^{1}*Moreover, brethren, I would not that ye should be ignorant, how that all our*

fathers were under the cloud, and all passed through the sea;
²And were all baptized unto Moses in the cloud and in the sea;
³And did all eat the same spiritual meat;
⁴And did all drink the same spiritual drink: for they drank of that spiritual Rock that followed them: and that Rock was Christ.   *(1 Corinthians 10:1-4)*

This Scripture explicitly states that the source of their spiritual nourishment was Christ. This occurred some 1,450 years before He was born as a human being. The Scripture says the Israelites ate spiritual food and drank spiritual drink. They were partaking of the same Christ that we partake of today at the Lord's Supper. The Lord was personally present to provide spiritual food and drink for an old covenant people. How much more is He personally present at His table for His new covenant people! *"He is the mediator of a better covenant, established upon better promises,"* as Hebrews 8:6 wonderfully asserts.

A third Scripture that attests to the truth of Jesus Christ's being personally present at the communion table is this:

²⁰When two or three are gathered together in my name there am I in the midst of them.   *(Matthew 18:20)*

Of all places, the Lord's Supper provides an ideal setting for Jesus Christ to be personally present among believers.

Doing God's will is *"doing"* the kingdom of God. His will is that we regularly participate in the Lord's Supper. When we do so, we may **expect** the Lord Jesus to be personally present.

Another author states a similar conclusion:

> If we take seriously the claim that the living Lord is the head of the church, his abiding presence would be known as often as believers met to share the fellowship meal. The Lord's Supper ritual may have varied...but the important element—the presence of the risen Christ in the company of the faithful—persisted. Apart from this vital and abiding element, it is difficult to account for the continuance and the centrality of the meal-rite in an emerging institutional Christianity.
>
> (Martin 1958, p. 6)

With Signs Following

I would tell my friend the second benefit of regularly partaking of the Lord's Supper is the expectation of *"signs following"* whenever she participates in the Lord's Supper. I would refer to the above Scriptures which describe Jesus as personally present when we are doing His will. Then, when Jesus is present, signs follow automatically. The laws of the kingdom of God override the laws of this world. That is why, I would explain, we may expect to be healed at the communion table.

I would hasten to remind her the converse of being in God's will while partaking of the Lord's table. The converse? *"For this reason many are weak and sickly among you, and many sleep"* (1 Corinthians 11:30). Several facts are presented in 1 Corinthians 11:17-34 which identify why those Christians were out of God's will when they partook of the Lord's Supper. These reasons include divisions, heresies, gluttony, selfishness, and drunkenness. It was those Christians, obviously out of the will of God, that Paul admonishes:

> [27]*Whosoever shall eat this bread, and drink this cup of the Lord, unworthily, shall be guilty of the body and blood of the Lord.*
> [28]*But let a man examine himself, and so let him eat of that bread, and drink of that cup.*
> [29]*For he that eateth and drinketh unworthily, eateth and drinketh damnation to himself, not discerning the Lord's body.*
> *(1 Corinthians 11:27-29)*

He then tells them point-blank, *"For this cause many are weak and sickly among you and many sleep"* (verse 30).

The remedy? Verses 31-34 tell them to judge themselves. That is, I believe, get right with God, with one another, and with themselves.

"In other words," I imagine my friend volunteering, "by doing the will of God, Christ is personally present, and we may expect signs to follow."

I would nod in agreement.

"In the case of the Lord's Supper," she would continue, "we may expect healings and miracles to occur as we partake of the elements."

I would nod again, adding, "And if we are out of God's will?"

"Why," she would exclaim, "the Bible plainly states what would happen. That is the reason why those people may likewise expect to be weak and sick."

"Is there a remedy?" I would prod her.

"Of course! Get in God's will!" she would retort.

"How does the kingdom of God relate to the Lord's Supper?" I would ask, hoping for a summary statement of the matter.

"I'll try," she would smile. "The kingdom of God is God's rule within our hearts. His kingdom operates by His spiritual laws. When we live out our lives according to His will and His laws, we may expect Jesus to be personally present with signs following.

"As for the relationship to the Lord's Supper," she would conclude, "we may then expect Jesus to be personally present, and, therefore, we may expect miracles and healings to take place among us."

"Sister," I would smile, "we have come a long way!"

Chapter 10

Jesus' Blood, Jesus' Body, My Healing

SUMMARY: *a comprehensive and usually brief abstract, recapitulation, or compendium of previously stated facts or statements.*

FAITH: *confidence or trust in a person or thing; belief that is not based on proof; belief in God or in the doctrines or teachings of religion; the trust in God and in His promises as made through Christ and the Scriptures by which man is justified or saved.*

D rawing the discussion with my friend in the blue dress to a close, I would say, "I think we are ready to summarize this whole discourse about the Lord's Supper."

"Any one of the three main topics would be enough for me," the woman in the blue dress would tactfully respond.

"The next time you take communion," I would continue, "meditate on how the Passover, the blood covenant, and the kingdom of God relate to what you are doing. Then, not only will you be looking backward to what Jesus did on the cross, and not only will you be looking forward to His second coming, but you will also be looking for His very presence in the communion service. In fact, you may expect to be healed while taking communion."

I can imagine her comment. "Do you remember what I said to you when I left church that Sunday when you preached and ministered communion?"

"Very well," I would recall. "You said that you never understood the healing part about the Lord's Supper. Or, another way of saying the same thing, you thought the Lord's Supper observed only Christ's death and His second coming. It was just a ritual you observed every Sunday.

"I really thank you for your honest comment," I would continue. "It hasn't been very long ago that I also searched out the Scriptures to understand the foundational truths underlying the Lord's Supper."

"Thank you for explaining what you have found out about those truths. Could you briefly summarize them?" she would ask.

Eager for the opportunity, I would answer, "I will try. And in doing so, I would also like to relate Jesus' body and blood to our healing."

The Passover

> [7]Christ, our Passover lamb, has been sacrificed. *(1 Corinthians 5:7 NIV)*

> [15]And he said unto them, with desire I have desired to eat this Passover with you before I suffer. *(Luke 22:15)*

An understanding of the Passover is one of the three foundations upon which the Lord's Supper is built. Why was it so important for Jesus to observe the Passover meal with His disciples the night before He was crucified? I believe the answer lies in three parts.

First, Jesus was crucified during the very day all of Jerusalem was celebrating the Passover. When the priests were killing the lambs for sacrifice, Jesus, the perfect Lamb of God, was made a perfect sacrifice for the whole world.

Second, by divine revelation, Paul says of Jesus, *"Christ, our Passover lamb"* where the word *"our"* refers to Christians. The new Passover replaced the old on that day.

Third, the sacrificed lambs in Egypt had provided deliverance and healing some 1,450 years earlier. The deliverance of the firstborn of the Israelites came by sprinkling blood of the lamb on the door frame. Physical healing came to all of them as they ate the sacrificed lamb to prepare them for the Exodus that very night. In an analogous way, our deliverance and healing was provided at the cross by Jesus, our Passover lamb.

"Christ, our Passover lamb" is for us today. How do we appropriate Jesus' blood and His body in the Lord's Supper?

I have found the best way to exercise my faith concerning *"Christ, our Passover lamb"* is to compare myself with the Israelite slave in Egypt the evening before the Exodus. He acted on the basis of verbal instructions passed down from God to Moses and from Moses on down the chain of command to some 2.5 million people. It must have seemed crazy to the slave to be told to kill his best lamb, sprinkle its blood over the door frame, and then to eat all of it including its entrails! Yet, to do so would mean his firstborn would be saved from death, and his whole family would be healed physically. To ignore the instructions would mean sickness and death.

How much easier we have it today as born-again Christians. Our instructions are written. We do not literally have to kill a lamb and sprinkle its blood and eat its flesh. We have *"Christ, our Passover lamb."* Recall that Jesus was introduced as the Lamb of God by John the Baptist. Also, the Scriptures state He was the Lamb who was slain before the world was created (Revelation 13:8).

So, when I take communion, I receive the elements by faith in what they represent. When I hear the words, *"take, eat; this is my body which is broken for you"* (1 Corinthians 11:24), I receive the bread by faith in Jesus' written command that I am to take it, that I am to eat it, and that it represents His body broken for me. Believing this by faith in the written Word, I receive the bread for my healing.

Likewise, when I hear the words, *"This cup is the new testament in my blood, which is shed for you"* (Luke 22:20), I receive the cup by faith in Jesus' written command that it represents His blood shed for me. Believing this, I receive it as a reminder of my salvation and the remission of my sins (Matthew 26:28).

My faith is in Jesus' written commands. I act on them in peace and joy and receive deliverance and healing. The Israelite slave placed his faith in verbal commands. He undoubtedly acted on them in fear and trembling, but nevertheless received deliverance and healing. Just as the Israelites celebrated the Passover every year, we as Christians *"proclaim the*

Lord's death till He comes" (1 Corinthians 11:26) every time we partake of communion.

What does it mean to "*proclaim the Lord's death*"? What is there to proclaim (declare, announce, expound) about the Lord's death? What would you say to someone who asked you about the meaning of Jesus' death?

In the context of the Passover, we would answer that His death means our deliverance and our healing. The cup and the bread represent forgiveness of sins and healing for the body. "*Christ, our Passover lamb*" is a perfect sacrifice.

We may conclude in a more general way that we are triune beings as stated clearly in the Scriptures:

> [23]*I pray God your whole* **spirit** *and* **soul** *and* **body** *be preserved blameless unto the coming our Lord Jesus Christ.*
> *(1 Thessalonians 5:23)*

When we partake of the Lord's Supper, we partake of His provision for our every need— spirit, soul, and body.

The Blood Covenant

> [25]*This cup is the new covenant in my blood.* *(1 Corinthians 11:25 NIV)*

[16]The cup of blessing which we bless, is it not the communion of the blood of Christ?
(1 Corinthians 10:16)

An understanding of the blood covenant i another foundation upon which the Lord' Supper is built. Why did Jesus say, *"This cuj is the new covenant in my blood"*? We have jus seen that He referred to the Passover when H said, *"Take, eat; this is my body which is brc ken for you"* (1 Corinthians 11:24). Then, at th same table a moment later, He introduced th words, *"This cup is the new covenant in m blood."*

One of the main blessings of the new cove nant, established by the shed blood of Jesu Christ, is that we are beneficiaries of that cove nant when we become Christians. We do **noth ing** to earn the right to become an heir unde the new covenant. We are like Mephibosheth Jonathan's son. He didn't deserve to be mad as one of King David's sons, but he had th **right** to be so. Why? He was a beneficiary of covenant made between his father and Davic The covenant was made before he was ever born. Likewise, we don't deserve to be *"heirs c God,"* but we have the **right** to be so. What i the basis of such a blessing? It is a blood cove nant instituted by Jesus. This covenant wa made before we were born.

When we partake of the Lord's Supper, we are reminded that the cup represents a new covenant. And we dare not forget that this new covenant is qualified by the words, *"in my blood."* The establishing of this covenant was certainly not an easy or trivial thing for God to do. *"God was in Christ, reconciling the world unto himself"* (11 Corinthians 5:19). Jesus, the Christ, was 100 percent God and 100 percent man. We can think of the innocent blood of God being shed as Jesus represented Him. I say this because God's blood is referred to in Acts 20:28: *"...feed the church of God, which he hath purchased with his own blood."* We can also think of our blood being shed as Jesus represented us as 100 percent man.

By the precious blood of Jesus, God has sealed a new covenant—a blood covenant—with us. By that covenant, God has made us His own children, bound to Him forever, and there is nothing, absolutely nothing, that can ever separate us from Him (Romans 8:38-39).

His blood, His body, my healing. How do we exercise our faith regarding the blood covenant when we partake of communion? I find that it helps my faith to consider Mephibosheth at King David's table. Everything, including servants, was provided for him as long as he lived. The reason? A blood covenant. His part to play? Mephibosheth had to believe what King David told him about the covenant. Then he had to accept it was for him. Then he had to act it out by moving into the king's palace and receiving all that was provided.

We, too, must believe and act. We must believe that we are beneficiaries of the new covenant. We then use our faith to receive all that God has provided.

When I am in a communion service, I meditate on Jesus' words that the cup is a reminder of the new covenant He has established in His blood. As a beneficiary of that covenant, I then use my faith to appropriate blessings provided by that covenant.

As for healing, I know that Jesus has provided physical healing as a result of the new covenant. For it is written, *"By whose stripes you were healed"* (1 Peter 2:24). I meditate on the fact that healing has been provided by Jesus when He shed His blood for me at the whipping post.

Consider the word *"communion"* in the Scripture:

> *16The cup of blessing which we bless, is it not the communion of the blood of Christ? The bread which we break, is it not the communion of the body of Christ?*
> *(1 Corinthians 10:16)*

It is translated from the Greek word *koinonia* from which many beautiful concepts arise when applied to participating in the Lord's Supper. Besides communion, *koinonia* may be translated as: having in common; partnership; fellowship; and association.

Very strong meanings are revealed in this Scripture when we use these words. For example, *"communion of the blood of Christ"* becomes *"partnership in the blood of Christ."* That is the basic, underlying concept of a blood covenant. A partnership is working together and sharing one another's resources. Therefore, being a partner in the blood of Christ means that all the benefits provided by that blood belong to us. What a basis for faith! As Christians, we are partners in the blood of Christ. So, when we partake in the Lord's Supper in a worthy manner, we exercise faith in our position as a partner in the blood covenant. This powerful relationship provides our needs as we work with God in carrying out His will on earth.

The Kingdom of God

[16]For I say unto you, I will not any more eat thereof, until it be fulfilled in the kingdom of God.   (Luke 22:16)

*¹⁸For I say unto you, l will not drink of the
fruit of the vine, until the kingdom of God
shall come.*   *(Luke 22:18)*

The reality of the kingdom of God is clearly
stated by Jesus in his institution of the Lord's
Supper. Matthew and Mark mention it in relation to drinking the *"fruit of the vine."* Luke's
gospel does the same and also adds the reference of eating the Passover in relation to the
kingdom of God.

Why did Jesus introduce the kingdom of
God in the Lord's Supper? Why is it necessary
that we understand the kingdom of God to
more fully participate in communion?

We know that the kingdom of God statement by Jesus evoked very strong emotions
within the men around that table the night
before He was crucified. For we read, *"And
there was also a strife among them, which of
them should be accounted the greatest"* (Luke
22:24). This occurred **after** the two references
by Jesus to the kingdom of God. We find similar interest being expressed several weeks later
in another reference to the kingdom of God by
our resurrected Lord. (See Acts 1:1-8.)

John's gospel does not include the Upper
Room account of the Lord's Supper. However,
the sixth chapter of John is a remarkable
chapter alluding to the Lord's Supper one year
before it actually was instituted. In it is a

reference that does not explicitly mention the kingdom of God but certainly implies it. Jesus said:

> [56]*He that eateth my flesh, and drinketh my blood, dwelleth in me and I in him.*
> *(John 6:56)*

This is the essence of the kingdom of God—Jesus in us and we in Him. The same truth was expressed by Paul years later, *"I live, yet not I but Christ liveth in me"* (Galatians 2:20).

How does my faith relate to the kingdom of God and thereby to the Lord's Supper? As Paul continued in Galatians 2:20, *"The life which I now live in the flesh l live by the faith of the Son of God, who loved me, and gave himself for me."* The life we live in the here and now is to be lived by faith. Faith in what? Faith in whom? One translation says:

> [20]*True, I am living, here and now, this mortal life, but my real life is the faith I have in the Son of God, who loved me, and gave himself for me.*
> *(Galatians 2:20 KNOX)*

Our faith is in Jesus Christ, the Son of God. Faith in Jesus can be more specifically considered faith in His blood. Back to the question at hand: "How does my faith in Jesus relate to the kingdom of God and thereby to the Lord's Supper?" The answer is clearly stated in the sixth chapter of John, which contains 71 verses, far too many to list here. Please read them and notice the following events:

1. The Jewish festival of the Passover was near (verse 4). Jesus would be crucified in exactly one year at the next Passover.

2. Jesus feeds the 5,000 (verses 5-14).

3. Jesus walks on the water (verses 15-21).

4. Upon seeing and experiencing these miracles, the people asked the same question that we ask Him today, *"What shall we do, that we might work the works of God?"* (verse 28).

5. Jesus' rather unexpected answer is worthy of a separate point in this list of events: *"Jesus answered and said unto them, this is the work of God that you believe in him whom he has sent"* (verse 29). The key is belief in the person of Jesus Christ. This principle is restated in John 14:12 as *"Verily,*

verily, I say unto you, He that believeth on me, the works that I do shall he do also; and greater works than these shall he do; because I go unto my Father." The doing comes after the believing.

6. The people asked for a sign that they may see and believe (verse 30). This question was asked after the feeding of the 5,000 and after Jesus walked on the water!

7. Jesus answered them with the *"I am the bread of life"* discourse (verses 31-58, 62-63). Notice that Jesus' answer increases in intensity. First He talked of manna, then of His flesh, then of His flesh and blood. It is the flesh and blood of Jesus that we as believers celebrate in the Lord's Supper.

8. Verse 56 speaks of the kingdom of God in relation to the Lord's Supper, *"He that eateth my flesh, and drinketh my blood, dwelleth in me, and I in him."* It is this verse that I just compared with Galatians 2:20.

9. Now for the decision we all face: *"From that time many of his disciples went back, and walked no more with him"* (verse 66). Or, *"Lord, to whom shall we go? Thou hast the words of eternal life. And we believe and are sure that thou art that Christ, the Son of the living God"* (verses 68-69).

Through the years I have often asked the Lord a similar question, "What shall I do, that I might work the works of God?" I can say I never came away from such a honest question with a list of things to do—go to the mission field, go start up a church, go on a fast, and so on. The answer always pointed me to Jesus, *"This is the work of God, that ye believe on Him whom he hath sent."*

At first, I experienced what these people must have experienced. It was easy to believe on Jesus because of the miracles He did. I was on the outside looking at His works through the New Testament account. Really, it was more of a belief in a historical Jesus.

Then, as I matured in the Word, the kingdom of God concept became more and more real to me. That is, I began to realize that Jesus, through the Holy Spirit, actually lived in me and I in Him. My belief *"on him whom he hath sent"* expanded to an experiential awareness of Jesus within me.

Now, at the present time, my belief in Jesus in relation to the Lord's Supper is based on His own statement:

> [63]*It is the spirit that quickeneth; the flesh profiteth nothing; the words that I speak unto you, they are spirit, and they are life.* (John 6:63)

As I believed on Jesus and experienced Him within me, I came to the place where His words became spirit and life. That is, Jesus' words about His flesh and blood make the Lord's Supper so meaningful. When He says *"eat my flesh"* and *"drink my blood,"* these words *"are spirit, and they are life."* Jesus' words to me are, in effect, "My Spirit and Life will enter you if you eat My flesh; My Spirit and Life will enter you if you drink My blood."

Believing and acting on Jesus' words that *"they are spirit, and they are life,"* thereby floods my human spirit with His Spirit and His Life. Therefore, in the Lord's Supper, provision is made for the kingdom of God to become active and powerful in the world through me.

We are to believe on Jesus as a Person within us. Then as we celebrate the Lord's Supper, Jesus is also celebrating the Lord's Supper within us by imparting His Spirit and Life to us. This impartation empowers us to assist God in carrying out His plans and purposes on the earth today. This is the kingdom of God in action.

More than a Ritual

"I see something in your summaries," my friend would volunteer with a sparkle in her eye. "May I share it?"

"By all means, go ahead."

"The **Passover** represents Jesus as our sacrificial Lamb. He was actually sacrificed for our deliverance and healing.

"The **blood covenant** identifies Jesus as taking our place in making a blood covenant with God. His humanity represented us and His divinity represented God in establishing the new covenant.

"The **kingdom of God** reveals Jesus as God within us to empower us for His work on the earth.

"So, when we observe the Lord's Supper, we are incorporating Jesus as our sacrifice, Jesus as our representative, and Jesus as our source of power."

"I really appreciate that insight," I would exclaim. "You have verbalized something that is very helpful to me."

"What is that?"

"The Passover and the blood covenant are historical. They are past tense. It is Jesus within us that makes the kingdom of God in the now, in the present tense today."

"I think I see what you are getting at," she would acknowledge. "But could you elaborate further?"

"Okay. For years, whenever I participated in a communion service, I always looked backward in time to the cross because of the Scripture, *'This do in remembrance of me.'* In addition, I always looked forward in time to the rapture by observing the Scripture, *'For as often as you eat this bread, and drink this cup, you do show the Lord's death till he come'* (1 Corinthians 11:24-26). These Scriptures are to be obeyed. We are to be in *'remembrance'* and anticipate *'till he come.'* Yet, my spirit seemed to expect something at the time I was taking communion. That expectation is the realization of Jesus within me to empower me for service in the kingdom of God."

"That is exciting. In the communion service we are to be energized anew to do God's will."

"That is what I am trying to say," I would smile. "The Lord's Supper is not only a memorial service. It is a time of receiving Jesus' Spirit and Life so that we may be equipped for service in the kingdom of God."

"I suppose if you ever wrote a book about this, you would title it, *The Lord's Supper, More Than a Ritual.*"

"I suppose I would!"

Chapter 11

The Lord's Supper

LORD'S SUPPER: *the sacrament in commemoration of the Last Supper; communion; mass; Eucharist.*

LAST SUPPER: *the Supper of Jesus and His disciples on the eve of His Crucifixion.*

A t this point, I would encourage my friend in the blue dress to volunteer to summarize the entire discussion of the Lord's Supper. I would tease her, saying, "I've taken so long, see how short you can make it!"

She would smile, think for a long moment, and then say something like, "The Bible represents the Lord's Supper as a memorial to the death of Jesus Christ and as our participation in the benefits of that death. The benefits are built on the foundations of *'Christ, our Passover lamb,'* the blood covenant, and the kingdom of God. One such benefit of partaking of the Lord's Supper is healing for our physical bodies. Another is empowering us for carrying out God's will on the earth."

"That is an excellent short summary," I would compliment her. "And would you believe that while you were speaking, I have thought of something else!"

"What now?" she would rightfully question."

"I see a danger here," I would say as I begin to find words to express myself. "It has to do with taking the Lord's Supper to obtain more spiritual favor. That is, mere observance of the Lord's Supper is not to be regarded as conferring God's grace on the participant."

"Go on," she would encourage me to elaborate.

"We as believers partake of the benefits of Christ's death all the time," I would continue. "The danger lies in making the Lord's Supper an aid to faith. It should be the other way around. That is, our faith should appropriate the memorial and the benefits of the Lord's Supper."

"I get the drift of what you are trying to say, but can you give me an example?"

"The most obvious example I can think of is that a person must be a Christian before he can take communion," I would respond. "That is, grace is not conferred on unbelievers to be saved at the Lord's Supper. We don't tell unbelievers to take communion in order to be saved."

"I have always understood that," she would say. "Can you give another example?"

"I'll give one that involves Christians. Each participant is asked to examine himself as to whether or not he can partake of the Lord's Supper in a worthy manner. What would be some reasons why a Christian should not participate of the Supper? I can think of three: first, Christians who fall into sin (1 Corinthians 5:11-13, 11 Thessalonians 3:6, 11-15); second, Christians who teach false doctrine (11 John 10-11, Titus 3:10); and third, Christians who promote divisions and dissensions (Romans 16:17). Christians who do these things and yet partake of the Lord's Supper do so in an *unworthy manner* with judgment following (1 Corinthians 11:27-32 NIV)."

"That is heavy," she would exclaim.

"I know it. We need to be right with God, with one another, and with ourselves. Again, taking communion in an *unworthy manner* will not confer grace on us. In fact, it brings judgment."

"Really," she would think out loud, "since Jesus is personally present at the communion table, do people think they can fool God?"

"Apparently they think that He doesn't know their thoughts or intentions. Did you

123

notice these verses in John 6?" I would question.

> ⁶⁴*But there are some of you that believe not. For Jesus knew from the beginning who they were that believed not, and who should betray him.*
> ⁷⁰*Jesus answered them, Have not I chosen you twelve, and one of you is a devil?*
> ⁷¹*He spake of Judas Iscariot the son of Simon: for he it was that should betray him, being one of the twelve.*
>
> *(John 6:64, 70-71)*

"Jesus knew from the beginning that Judas would betray him," I emphasized. "And furthermore, Judas' taking the Lord's Supper in the Upper Room did not automatically confer grace on him that he would be suddenly transformed from a 'devil' to a 'saint'!"

"Taking communion is a serious thing," she would continue to reflect. "How does it relate to baptism?"

"I feel baptism should precede the Lord's Supper, but it is not mandatory that it must. There just isn't any Scripture relating baptism to the Lord's Supper. Communion is for Christians everywhere who are in right standing with God, their fellow man, and themselves." I would add, "You can receive communion at anytime, anywhere. You don't have to go to a church building to observe the Lord's Supper."

Crackers and Grape Juice

"What about crackers and grape juice?" she would continue. "I've always been served a little cracker and a little plastic cup of grape juice for communion. However, my Catholic friend is given a thin round wafer. And I have another friend whose church uses alcoholic wine. What do you feel is right?"

"Believe me, I have questioned this, too. I am also very much aware that the elements used in the Lord's Supper are an emotional issue with many Christians.

"I feel the spiritual meaning of the Lord's Supper is far more important than the physical elements we use to celebrate it. In other words, a good understanding of the Passover, the blood covenant, and the kingdom of God is most important when we take communion. Thus, an understanding of these three concepts should take precedence over the consideration of the physical elements we use."

"I understand and agree with you. But what elements do you recommend?" she would ask again.

"Okay. Okay. I will try to be more specific. The Greek word translated 'bread' should have been rendered 'loaf.' In other words, we could read Jesus'*took a loaf* as in Matthew 26:26. Likewise, the *'breaking of bread'* of Acts 2:42 and 46 was the breaking (not cutting) of a loaf of bread. And when Jesus said *'fruit of the vine'* as in Mark 14:25, we can understand that as reference to either fresh grape juice or alcoholic wine made from fermented grapes."

"But I still have questions about the elements we should use. Can you be more specific?"

"Yes, and I believe I have a lead to an answer. Two interesting facts arise from Jesus' words recorded in Luke 22:15: *'With desire I have desired to eat this Passover with you before I suffer.'*

"Jesus and His disciples were celebrating the annual Passover as they had undoubtedly done every year. (See Mark 14:12-16.) Therefore, if we can find out the nature of the *'loaf'* and of *'the fruit of the vine'* used in the Passover celebration in His day, we can answer your question."

Unleavened Bread

"The nature of the loaf Jesus used is clearly known from Exodus 12:14-20 where God instructed Moses and Aaron about the Passover observance. God specified the loaf of bread was to be made without leaven. Therefore, the loaf Jesus broke during the Passover meal was undoubtedly flat and somewhat hard because it had been baked without yeast.

"Why would Jesus use bread made without yeast? We know that yeast is used to introduce fermentation in the production of bread to cause it to rise or expand. We also know leaven or yeast typifies the spreading influence of corruption and evil as in the fifth chapter of 1 Corinthians. Therefore, I believe Jesus used unleavened bread not only to be in accordance with the law, but also to illustrate that no sin (leaven) had contaminated His body which the loaf represents."

The Fruit of the Vine

"The alcoholic content of the *'fruit of the vine'* is not explicitly specified in Scripture. I am talking about the institution of the Lord's Supper where Jesus used the words, *'fruit of the vine'* and not other Bible references to *'wine'* such as the miracle of turning water to wine or of Paul counseling Timothy to use a little wine for his stomach.

"The first insight on this subject comes from Jesus' words, *'I will drink no more of the fruit of the vine, until that day that I drink it new, in the kingdom of God'* (Mark 14:25). His words point to heaven and perhaps to *'the marriage supper of the lamb'* (Revelation 19:9) specifically. I can't imagine anything being fermented (contaminated, polluted, spoiled) in God's presence. Hence, I expect *the fruit of the vine* in heaven will be like pure grape juice.

"The second point that favors serving unfermented or nonalcoholic juice for communion is found in 1 Corinthians 8:9 (NAS). Paul warns us, *But take care lest this liberty of yours somehow become a stumbling block to the weak.* For us to introduce our saved children to alcohol or to tempt a person who has struggled to get free from the bondage of addiction by using alcoholic wine for communion doesn't line up with God's will.

"For these reasons, I recommend we use a loaf of unleavened bread and grape juice in our communion service."

A Common Cup

Another question would arise from her. "You forgot to say how the grape juice is to be served."

"The Scriptures imply a common cup," I would reply. *Drink ye, all of it* of Matthew 26:27 really should be translated *Drink from it, all of you* as in the New International Version. The first translation implies everyone is to drink all of the juice in his individual cup while the second means everyone is to drink from the same cup. Therefore, a common loaf and a common cup seems to me to be the way Jesus instituted the Lord's Supper.

"There is something else that needs to be said about the common cup. Everyone partaking from the same cup speaks of unity, togetherness, sharing. What comes first to unite a body of believers into true unity? Does the unity come first and then celebrated in communion by drinking of the same cup representing that unity? Or, would using the common cup with proper teaching at communion time help to instill unity within the body of believers?"

Details

A pause, a shrug of her shoulders, and again, another probe. "Do you feel what you are saying is the only way to observe communion?"

"Like I said before, I believe an understanding of the Passover, the blood covenant, and the kingdom of God in relationship to the Lord's Supper is more important than the physical considerations of whether to use a loaf or crackers, wine or juice, common or individual cups.

"To duplicate the physical characteristics of that first Lord's Supper in our day, we would also have to observe details like taking communion only at night, only in an upper room, and only after a meal. Of these three details, I really feel a meal should be involved. In fact, there is much more scriptural basis for celebrating the Lord's Supper in the context of a meal than after a preaching or teaching session as is so common in our day.

"May I suggest something?" I would seek to conclude these issues with my inquisitive friend.

"You asked me to summarize a few minutes ago. Now it's your turn," she would smile.

A Proposal

"When we observe the Lord's Supper in church or in our homes, why not break up into small groups of approximately twelve persons, like the number at the first Lord's Supper? Have one person administer a common loaf of unleavened bread and a common cup of grape juice within each group. In a church setting, the pastor could oversee the entire congregation divided up into these small groups and allow time for unity to develop within each group."

"That would set the stage for an intimate, scriptural observance of the Lord's table," she would reflect.

A Beautiful Experience

"The most meaningful communion I have experienced," I would volunteer, "is where I examined myself before the Lord and then made my way up to the leader of the service who was holding a loaf of bread and a cup of grape juice. I then broke off a small piece of bread from the loaf and dipped it into the cup of juice. Then, as I put the juice-soaked bread into my mouth, he quietly spoke something like, *'This is Jesus' body which was broken for you,'* and *'This is Jesus' blood which was shed for you.'* The bread was broken off from a loaf obviously made with yeast. And although a common cup was used, no one actually drank from it. But yet, that Lord's Supper was more than a ritual."

"Well, I know now that the Lord's Supper is certainly more than a ritual! It is even more than a memorial service," she would beam. "In fact, from now on, I'll use my faith to appropriate the benefits provided for me by the Passover, the blood covenant, and the kingdom of God."

"Yes, my friend, and it is my prayer that Christians the world over would practice the Lord's Supper in the holiness it deserves. It is like eating a meal in the very presence of the Lord Jesus Himself."

Last Words

"I found something interesting about the Lord's Supper that I would like to share before you leave," I would add. "It is from the *Heidelberg Catechism*, Question 76."

"Where did you find **that**?" she would openly wonder.

"I found it in a book by Andrew Murray called *The Power of the Blood of Jesus*. His personal view of the Lord's Supper coincided with the answer given to Question 76. He introduced the question with the comment, 'There is something more in the Supper than simply the believer appropriating the redemptive work of Christ' (Murray 1993, p. 142). Here, then, is the question and its answer:"

Heidelberg Catechism, Question 76

What is it then to eat the crucified body of Christ and to drink His shed blood?

It is not only to embrace with a believing heart all the sufferings and death of Christ, and thereby to receive pardon of sin and eternal life; but, also besides that, to become more and more united to His sacred body, by the Holy Spirit who dwells at once both in

Christ and in us; so that we, though
Christ is in heaven and we on earth,
are, notwithstanding, flesh of His flesh,
and bone of His bones; and we live and
are governed forever by one Spirit.

(Murray 1993, p. 142)

"That's good," she would comment. "And I
believe I can see elements of the Passover, the
blood covenant, and the kingdom of God in that
one short answer."

"You really catch on fast," I would compliment her.

"Thank you. This has been fun. But I
really need to be going," she would say, glancing at her watch.

"Have I kept you too long?"

"The time really has gone by fast," she
would tactfully respond. Then, with a sparkle
in her eyes, she would exclaim, "I can't wait
until I take communion next time!"

PART THREE:

Speaking Blood, Speaking Faith

Chapter 12

Of First Importance

Lester Sumrall, in speaking about the blood of Jesus, says:

> That is the most powerful thing in the universe—the blood of the Lord Jesus Christ.
>
> (Sumrall 1980)

Stanley H. Frodsham wrote about the blood of Jesus:

> Now, once again, the Lord is bringing the power of the blood to the attention of the Church. Let us honor and plead the blood of the Lamb very reverently; for through the blood we have power over all the might of the enemy. To those who, not mechanically, but in true holy reverence, plead the blood of the Lamb, there will be a restoration of all that the locust, the cankerworm, the caterpillar, and the palmerworm have eaten.
>
> (Frodsham 1973, p. 9)

H.A. Maxwell Whyte concluded his book, *The Power of the Blood,* with these words:

I believe that the Church has yet to discover the deeper dimension of spiritual warfare through pleading the Blood. Great miracles can take place if we learn this secret. There is wonder-working power in the Blood!

(Whyte 1973, p. 92)

The following quotations relate the cross and the blood:

The message of the cross and the power of the Blood of Jesus are the cornerstones of all Christendom. (Schoch 1964, p. 3)

'The cross' and 'the blood of Jesus' are indeed names for profound mysteries.

(Chambers 1984, p. 26)

As Christians, we realize the blood of Jesus Christ is the legal basis of our faith. Scriptures such as the following are familiar:

[17]*In whom we have redemption through his blood.* (Ephesians 1:17)
[7]*The blood of Jesus Christ his Son cleanseth us from all sin.* (1 John 1:7)

These verses clearly reveal that our salvation and cleansing from sins are based on the blood of Jesus. However, as we shall discover, we possess many other benefits provided by the blood.

Before we begin, I anticipate two questions that need to be dealt with. First, just how important is it that we study the blood of Jesus? Second, is the phrase "plead the blood of Jesus Christ" scriptural?

Why Study about the Blood?

Let's turn to 1 Corinthians 15:3-4 for an answer to the first question:

> ³For what I received I passed on to you as of first importance, that Christ died for our sins according to the Scriptures,
> ⁴that he was buried, that he was raised...
> (NIV)

Christ's death, burial, and resurrection are called **of first importance**. These fundamental truths were set forth by Paul to the church by supernatural revelation. Why do I call these a supernatural revelation? Because Paul did! In writing to Christians in the churches in Galatia, he said:

> ¹¹I want you to know, brothers, that the gospel I preached is not something that man made up.
> ¹²I did not receive it from any man, nor was I taught it; rather, I received it by revelation from Jesus Christ.
> (Galatians 1:11-12)

"That Christ died for our sins" is the part of the revelation that is preached and taught most frequently. And it is here that the Holy Spirit wants to reveal to us in a deeper way the meaning of the blood of Jesus Christ. It is a tremendous study. It is a study **of first importance.**

Why study about the blood? Another reason is because the Apostle Paul, in addressing the elders of the church at Ephesus, made a most remarkable statement. He said, in part:

> *²⁸Feed the church of God, which He hath purchased with His own blood.*
> *(Acts 20:28)*

Taken in context, this sentence structure clearly reveals that Paul is making reference to the very blood of God the Father. Verses like this remind me that I don't fully understand the mystery of the Trinity! We are considering the blood of God Himself. It was manifested in the human body of Jesus Christ. It was through Jesus that the precious blood of God purchased the church. Is a study of the blood important? Ask God the Father!

Is "Pleading the Blood" Scriptural?

This second question concerning "pleading the blood of Jesus" may best be answered by ministering in the spirit of the Word and not just the letter (11 Corinthians 3:6). First, the actual phrase "plead the blood" is not in the Bible. However, for one example among many others, neither is the phrase "Sunday school" in the Bible. But certainly the concept of our modern day Sunday school is implied in Scripture. I think of Colossians 1:10 as an example which states, *"...increasing in the knowledge of God."* Another example is 11 Timothy 2:15, *"Study to show thyself approved unto God."* I suppose there are dozens of similar Scriptures which give a basis for the existence of Sunday schools.

In a similar way, the words "plead the blood of Jesus" are not found in the Bible. Yet many Scriptures certainly imply that "pleading the blood" is a valid expression of our faith in that blood.

The purpose of this section of the book is to show what it means to "plead the blood of Jesus Christ." The blood is a study *"of first importance."* Let us begin at the beginning.

Chapter 13

Abel's Crying Blood

*And he said, What hast thou done? The voice
of thy brother's blood crieth unto me
from the ground.*
—*Genesis 4:10* KJV

*The Lord said, "What have you done? Listen!
Your brother's blood cries out to me
from the ground."*
—*Genesis 4:10* NIV

*And He said, "What have you done? The voice
of your brother's blood is crying to me
from the ground."*
—*Genesis 4:10* NAS

T hree different translations of this verse
reveal the amazing fact that the innocent
shed blood of Abel cried out to God from the
ground! This verse discloses that Abel's blood
has a voice, uses the voice to cry out, cries from
the ground, cries to God, and is heard by God.

We are delving into spiritual matters which cannot be understood by our natural human reasoning. It is not within the power of the natural mind to understand that blood can communicate with God. Yet, it is possible for things of God to be revealed to the Christian. The revelation is by the Holy Spirit. He is called Teacher, Guide, and Helper for this very reason.

Let me further illustrate the truth of speaking blood as a mystery of God by presenting Scripture found in 1 Corinthians:

> [6]*We speak wisdom among them that are perfect* [mature]: *yet not the wisdom of this world...*
> [7]*But we speak the wisdom of God in a mystery, even the hidden wisdom...*
> [10]*But God hath revealed them unto us by his Spirit: for the Spirit searcheth all things, yea, the deep things of God.*
> [11]*...the things of God knoweth no man, but the Spirit of God.*
> [12]*Now we have received, not the spirit of the world, but the Spirit which is of God, that we might know the things that are freely given to us of God.*
> [13]*Which things also we speak, not in the words which man's wisdom teacheth, but which the Holy Ghost teacheth; comparing spiritual things with spiritual.*

> [14]*But the natural man receiveth not the things of the Spirit of God: for they are foolishness unto him: neither can he know them, because they are spiritually discerned.* (1 Corinthians 2:6-7, 10-14)

These verses make it clear that things of God are only understood with help from the Spirit of God. Depending on the Holy Spirit to help us *"to come unto the knowledge of the truth"* (1 Timothy 2:4) about blood that speaks, let us proceed.

The Beginning

The principle of innocent blood being shed for the guilty begins in the Garden of Eden. God had created Adam, placed him in a perfect environment, and gave him authority over everything on earth (Genesis 1:26-28).

Before God made Eve, He told Adam *"thou shalt surely die"* if he disobeyed Him and ate of the tree of the knowledge of good and evil. After Eve was made, Adam certainly warned her of God's words to him. We know this because the serpent tempted her with reference to the very words God had spoken to Adam. He said, *"Hath God said, Ye shall not eat of every tree of the garden?"* and *"Ye shall not surely die"* (Genesis 3:1, 4). The serpent tempted Eve with the words God had given Adam. Both Adam and Eve disobeyed God, obeyed the devil, and initiated the fall of Man. Their act has separated every person from God since that time.

Adam and Eve immediately *"sewed fig leaves together, and made themselves aprons"* (Genesis 3:7). Notice that after God appeared and questioned the transgressors, He left their presence only after making them *"coats of skins, and clothed them"* (Genesis 3:21). In order to make coats of skins, an innocent animal was sacrificed. It was by this act that God instituted the principle of slaying the innocent for the guilty. It is evident that God had no regard for the clothes Adam and Eve made for themselves out of fig leaves.

An interesting conjecture arises at this point. Can you imagine Adam and Eve, cast out of the Garden and from the presence of God, saying to one another, "Why didn't God kill us? For He said *'in the day that thou eatest thereof thou shalt surely die'"* (Genesis 2:17). I can imagine them expecting to die the same day they ate the forbidden fruit, and yet nothing happened. (We realize that they died spiritually but not physically.)

Adam and Eve must have reasoned that since they were not struck dead, God must have made some provision that they could live. What was that provision? After recounting the events in the Garden dozens of times, they must have finally realized that the shedding of the blood of the innocent animal somehow appeased God from killing them. Two facts arise from this discovery: (1) the principle of innocent blood shed for the guilty was established, and (2) God required innocent blood to appease His wrath for sin. These facts are not popular. Man's natural tendency is to have a bloodless religion. Yet God's supernatural requirement is to require blood in man's approach to Him.

Believe Dad and Mom?

Cain and Abel were subsequently born as natural children to Adam and Eve. I imagine that with only four human beings on earth, the two sons grew up in very close relationship to their parents with plenty of time to talk about the Garden of Eden experience. It was a childhood without telephones, newspapers, television, and such, but with plenty of time for talking.

It is easy for me to imagine Adam and Eve repeatedly taught their sons during the years. It would seem that the "bottom line" of their instruction would have been something like the following: "God said if we disobeyed Him, we would surely die. But we are still living. The

147

only reason we can think why we are still alive is that the blood of an innocent animal shed for us somehow appeased God. Therefore, sons, if you want to approach God, we advise you to offer a sacrifice of blood from an innocent animal." I am saying that I believe Cain and Abel were taught this all their lives. But did they believe it?

Exam Time

The biblical account continues in the fourth chapter of Genesis:

> *³And in process of time it came to pass, that Cain brought of the fruit of the ground an offering unto the Lord.*
> *⁴And Abel, he also brought of the firstlings of his flock and of the fat thereof. And the Lord had respect unto Abel and to his offering:*
> *⁵But unto Cain and to his offering he had not respect.* (Genesis 4:3-5)

We see that Cain did not believe what his parents taught him, whereas Abel did. God rejected Cain's fruit and vegetable offering, because it was not a blood sacrifice. It appears that God gave him a second chance (verses 6 and 7), but Cain refused to change.

On the other hand, *"by faith Abel offered unto God a more excellent sacrifice than Cain"* (Hebrews 11:4). Abel's faith was in his parents' teaching. He obeyed them. He was a believer.

By approaching God his own way, Cain made his offering unto God. He disobeyed his parents' teaching. He was an unbeliever.

Our Turn

At this point one wonders, "How could Adam and Eve possibly disobey God?" and "How could Cain disobey his parents?" It brings me up short to find out that I, as a Christian, have a similar instruction to obey when approaching God. The Word of God, written for our instruction (11 Timothy 3:16), says:

> [19]*Having therefore, brethren, boldness to enter into the holiest by the blood of Jesus,* [22]*Let us draw near with a true heart in full assurance of faith.*
>
> *(Hebrews 10:19,22)*

Notice the key words: **brethren** (fellow Christians), **having boldness, enter into, the holiest** (God's very presence), **by the blood of Jesus** (no other way), **draw near, true heart, full assurance of faith.**

This instruction is for us today! No longer do I look backwards to put blame on Adam and Eve, Cain and Abel. Instructions like this now capture my attention in the day in which we are living on earth.

Whose Way?

A related Scripture, while it only implies the shed blood of Jesus Christ, was given by our Lord as He was describing the mansions in our Father's house in heaven:

> *⁶I am the way, the truth, and the life: no man cometh unto the Father, but by me.*
> *(John 14:6)*

The point I want to emphasize here is the same that Cain in his day and many millions in our day wrestle with. It is, "Do we approach God our way or by God's way?" God's way is through the shed blood of His sacrificial Son, Jesus Christ. Consider the millions and millions of people who are trying to satisfy their heart hunger for God by participating in man's religion, in man's approach to God. What a call for evangelism! For teaching! For missions! The only approach to God is through Jesus Christ by virtue of His shed blood. We must worship God in His revealed way. His revelation includes appropriating (taking for oneself; taking possession of) the blood of Jesus.

An Example

To give a personal example, ever since I discovered these Scriptures, my approach to God the Father is to pray something like this: "Father God, I come before you on the basis of the shed blood of Jesus Christ, your Son and my Savior and Lord..." This approach to God is by my believing the Word is true and acting on it (a definition of faith). I almost always have the above verses in mind when I begin praying. Many times I find myself being so thankful that I don't have to go to all the time and trouble to make a literal blood sacrifice of an animal or bird in my approach to God. I recall Jesus' finished work for me:

> [12]*Neither by the blood of goats and calves, but by His own blood he entered in once into the holy place, having obtained eternal redemption for us.* (Hebrews 9:12)

Again, I believe and act on what the Word reveals. My spirit is satisfied that there is nothing I need to do by any physical activity to approach God. I appropriate what Jesus has already done.

Cain Murders Abel

Cain's offering was rejected by God. Abel's was accepted. Cain did not respond as God required. The issue is the same today. There are two ways to approach God—man's way and God's way.

After God literally spoke to Cain, then *"Cain talked with Abel his brother"* (Genesis 4:8). The margin rendering in my Bible for *"talked"* is the word "quarreled." Perhaps the quarrel centered around how to approach God. In any case, Cain's heart was hardened against God's way. In a rage of jealousy, he killed his brother.

Then a most amazing phenomenon happened. As our text verse in three translations for this chapter explicitly points out, Abel's blood cried out to God from the ground! Abel was innocent. God heard Abel's blood crying out to Him. Once more God talked with Cain, and again it appears Cain hardened his heart to God, because we read in the New Testament, *"Woe unto them! for they have gone in the way of Cain"* (Jude 11).

Is this account of God's watch care over innocent blood limited only to Cain and Abel? Or, are there other scriptural accounts involving blood that will help establish the principle of innocent blood being shed for the guilty? Of course, we know this principle was ultimately manifested in Jesus Christ at the cross. However, before we discuss Jesus and His shed blood, let us consider another example of innocent blood being shed.

Noah

Some 1600 years passed between Cain and Abel's day and Noah's flood. Chapters four through six of Genesis tell how sin multiplied rapidly and was very great. In fact, sin was so prevalent that God destroyed all living creatures except eight people and the animals and fowl with them in the ark.

It is very significant that Noah offered burnt offerings to God as soon as the ark was emptied after the flood (Genesis 8:19-21). I believe Noah was the only righteous man on earth just before the flood (Genesis 6:8 and 7:1). And I believe the evidence for this statement is that Noah worshiped God as He required. We see Noah worshiping God like this:

> [20]And Noah builded an altar unto the Lord; and took of every clean beast, and of every clean fowl, and offered burnt offerings on the altar.   (Genesis 8:20)

The blood of innocent animals and fowl was shed to provide a burnt offering to the

Lord. God certainly accepted Noah's worship (Genesis 8:21-9:19). Notice God's own language concerning blood:

> ⁴*Flesh with the life thereof, which is the blood thereof, shall ye not eat.*
> ⁵*And surely your blood of your lives will I require; at the hand of every beast will I require it, and at the hand of man; at the hand of every man's brother will I require the life of man.*
> ⁶*Whoso sheddeth man's blood, by man shall his blood be shed: for in the image of God made he man.*   (Genesis 9:4-6)

To paraphrase, I believe God's view of human and animal blood is along these lines:

1. The life, or life force, is in the blood.
2. God is the sole Lord of all life.
3. He is sovereign over the blood and life of men.
4. Hence, He avenges the shedding of innocent human blood.
5. Animal blood also belongs to God. It is holy (because it was used as a holy offering to God), and therefore the consumption of blood is forbidden on pain of death.

It is interesting to note that, centuries later, when the apostles boiled down all the

Jewish customs which new Gentile Christians must obey, two of the four prohibited drinking blood (Acts 15:20, 29). In God's eyes, blood of men and animals is very important. How much more must be His own blood manifested through His only Son, Jesus Christ (Acts 20:28)!

Chapter 14

Jesus' Speaking Blood

*[Jesus'] blood of sprinkling, that speaketh
better things than that of Abel.*
—Hebrews 12:24

We have seen that Abel's blood speaks. Also
our text verse plainly states that Jesus'
blood speaks. Furthermore, taken in context,
this Scripture elevates the speaking blood of
Jesus to be in the same class as God, Jesus,
angels, the church, and the spirits of righteous
men! Let me outline this fact found in Hebrews:

> ¹⁸*Ye are not come unto the mount that
> might be touched, and that burned with
> fire, nor unto blackness, and darkness, and
> tempest,*
> ¹⁹*And the sound of a trumpet, and the
> voice of words; which voice they that heard
> in treated that the word should not be
> spoken to them any more:*
> ²⁰*(For they could not endure that which
> was commanded, And if so much as a*

beast touch the mountain, it shall be
stoned, or thrust through with a dart:
²¹And so terrible was the sight, that Moses
said, I exceedingly fear and quake:)
                              (Hebrews 12:18-21)

Notice this description of God's presence on
Mt. Sinai registered on man's physical senses
as touch, smell, sight, and hearing. In fact, the
one word *"tempest"* would be enough to describe
what was happening. Its dictionary definition
makes this clear:

> **TEMPEST:** *an extreme current of*
> *wind rushing with great velocity and*
> *violence, especially one attended with*
> *rain, hail, or snow; a violent storm; a*
> *violent commotion, disturbance, or*
> *tumult.*

So terrible was the sight that Moses said,
"I exceedingly fear and quake." This is the same
Moses who had talked with God face to face on
the same mountain for forty days and nights.
The physical manifestations of God's anger
were so great that Moses was filled with fear.

Thank God that we do not approach Him
in such a manner! This is how we approach
God as New Testament believers:

158

²²But ye are come unto mount Sion, and unto the city of the living God, the heavenly Jerusalem, and to an innumerable company of angels,
²³To the general assembly and church of the firstborn, which are written in heaven, and to God the Judge of all, and to the spirits of just men made perfect,
²⁴And to Jesus the mediator of the new covenant, and to the blood of sprinkling, that speaketh better things than that of Abel. (Hebrews 12:22-24)

God's habitation is called the heavenly Jerusalem. Now, what do we find in this city of the living God?

1. An innumerable company of angels,
2. The church of the firstborn,
3. God, the Judge of all,
4. The spirits of just men made perfect,
5. Jesus, the mediator of a new covenant, and
6. The blood of sprinkling that speaketh.

The speaking blood of Jesus is found in heaven! Since we know God, Jesus, angels, and the church are living and are in heaven, and since the blood of Jesus is cataloged in the same list, it follows that the blood is also alive

159

and in heaven. Furthermore, the blood is speaking. Let us consider these marvelous facts in greater detail.

The Blood Is Alive in Heaven

The fact that the blood of Jesus is in heaven is also documented elsewhere. We know that Christ *"by his own blood entered in once into the holy place, having obtained eternal redemption for us"* (Hebrews 9:12).

Jesus, at His ascension on resurrection morning, entered the holy place by His own blood and presented Himself before God the Father. The Father accepted the blood. Jesus thereby *"obtained eternal redemption for us."* From this passage we know the blood of Jesus is in heaven.

Hebrews 10:20 describes the blood of Jesus as *"a new and living way."* Wonder of wonders, that blood is alive! It is in the same list, and therefore in the same class of existence as God, Jesus, angels, and the church! We know they are alive today. Therefore, we know the blood of Jesus is alive today.

The concept of living blood in heaven may at first glance appear too extreme. But consider these other living entities which are mentioned in Scripture:

1. Living water (John 4:10-11),
2. Living bread (John 6:51),
3. Living stones (1 Peter 2:4),
4. Living fountains of waters (Revelation 7:17), and
5. Living word (Hebrews 4:12).

Indeed, there are other spiritual manifestations recorded in Scripture which are unknown in the physical realm monitored by our five senses. For example, recall Jesus' startling statement that stones could be made to cry out (Luke 19:40), and John the Baptist's declaration that God is able to raise up children unto Abraham from stones (Luke 3:8). In the same way, the blood of Jesus is living. And it is speaking.

The Blood Is Speaking

What is the blood of Jesus speaking? The Word says that it is speaking *better things than that of Abel*" (Hebrews 12:24). Abel's blood cried out to God from the ground. Abel's blood undoubtedly cried out for vengeance. And I believe the *"better things"* of Jesus' speaking blood would be in line with His perfect character. That is, His blood is speaking forgiveness, love, grace, mercy, and such.

161

Yes, Jesus' blood is still speaking today. And I believe it is speaking for our benefit. It is not limited just to those responsible for His crucifixion where He said, *"Father forgive them, for they know not what they do"* (Luke 23:34). This limited application would only parallel Abel's blood as it cried out when he was murdered by his brother. No, the Greek word translated in Hebrews 12:24 as *"speaketh"* (KJV), and *"speaks"* (NIV and NAS), is a present tense verb that means the blood of Jesus is continuously speaking. It is speaking for everyone that Christ died for—you and me and everyone who has ever been born. The blood is speaking *"better things"* than that of Abel's blood. It speaks *"better things"* like forgiveness, love, grace, and mercy.

Other Voices

The blood is speaking today. And there are other heavenly voices speaking all the time. We are in the middle of a spiritual tug-of-war! On one side, the Holy Spirit *"maketh intercession for us... according to the will of God"* (Romans 8:26-27). With Him, *"Christ...also maketh intercession for us"* (Romans 8:34), and *"[Jesus] ever liveth to make intercession for them"* (Hebrews 7:25). The very Bible word *"intercession"* is powerful. As used with the Holy Spirit it means, "to meet with in behalf of one." As used with Jesus it means, "to meet with, come between, intercede." The dictionary definition for *intercede* contains the word "plead" which we will use later on for "plead the blood." The definition is:

> **INTERCEDE:** *to plead or petition in behalf of one in difficulty or trouble.*

For the sake of completeness, a dictionary definition for intercession is:

> **INTERCESSION:** *a prayer to God on behalf of another or others.*

From these definitions, it is obvious that the Holy Spirit and Jesus are interceding with God on behalf of us.

On the other side of the tug-of-war in the heavenlies concerning us, the devil is also very active, for it is yet in the future that:

> *[10]The accuser* [the devil] *of our brethren is cast down, which accused them before our God day and night.* (Revelation 12:10)

This says that Satan is accusing us before God day and night!

Jesus speaks **for** us. The Holy Spirit speaks **for** us. The devil speaks **against** us. It should be no surprise to discover that the blood also speaks and that it speaks for us.

I am so thankful that Jesus *"ever liveth"* to make intercession for us. This means He is waging a continual ministry of intercession to combat the devil's day and night accusations. We know Jesus has already defeated the devil, so if we submit to Jesus as our Lord each day, we know His intercessions completely overwhelm the devil's accusations. Thank you Jesus for ever living to make intercession for us!

No Contest

My first reaction to the spiritual tug-of-war in heaven over me was something like, "Two against one—no contest!" That is true. The Holy Spirit and Jesus versus the devil is no contest. However, something within me said there should be the Trinity on my side. I searched the Scriptures and found an answer:

> *7For there are three that bear record in heaven, the Father, the Word, and the Holy Ghost: and these three are one.*
> *(1 John 5:7)*

"The Word" is a synonym for Jesus Christ (John 1:1-5). The clause *"These three are one"* is a very clear statement in Scripture that speaks

164

of the Trinity of God. Therefore, this verse satisfies my spirit that God the Father is also active on my behalf in heaven. Now it is "Three against one—no contest!"

Our Part

We have a part to play in this spiritual tug-of-war raging about us. We cannot be passive about it. We must choose sides. The Old Testament said:

> [15]*Choose you this day whom ye will serve...*
> *but as for me and my house, we will serve*
> *the Lord.* (Joshua 24:15)

The New Testament's counterpart is a stronger command:

> [7]*Submit yourselves therefore to God. Resist*
> *the devil, and he will flee from you.*
> (James 4:7)

Let us submit ourselves completely to God. Tell Him so. Let us resist the devil. Tell him so. The Word says then the devil will flee from us. With our decision to enter the tug-of-war on God's side, it is now "Four against one—no contest!"

I have said all this to make this point: there are voices in heaven speaking about everyone of us. They range from the intercessions of the Trinity to the accusations of the devil. With this background, it should not be so surprising that the blood of Jesus Christ is also in heaven speaking *"better things"* on our behalf.

Where We Are

We now have an inkling of what it means to "plead the blood." What we know at this point is that the blood of Jesus is alive; is in heaven with God, Jesus, angels, Old Testament saints, and the church; is speaking; and is speaking *"better things."*

The blood of Jesus is alive and is speaking in heaven. The next task is to find out just what the blood is speaking.

What Is the Blood Saying?

I believe several things should be clear at this point about the speaking blood of Jesus.

First of all, it speaks *"better things"* for our benefit just as Jesus *"ever liveth to make intercession for them"* is for our benefit.

Secondly, we cannot separate Jesus and His blood. Together, they are the foundation of the entire Bible. Scriptures like, *"the Lamb slain from the foundation of the world"* (Revelation 13:8), and *"[we] were redeemed...with the precious blood of Christ"* (1 Peter 1:18-19), immediately come to mind. Therefore, we can conclude that Jesus' blood is speaking the same kind of things for our benefit that Jesus Himself in His present day ministry is interceding for our benefit.

Third, we will be immeasurably helped by setting ourselves in agreement with what the blood is speaking on our behalf. Recall James 4:7 again, *"Submit yourselves to God. Resist the devil and he will flee from you."* Let us purpose in our hearts to submit to God and to resist the devil's attempts to keep us from appropriating the blood for our benefit.

Fourth, we need to *"search the Scriptures"* (Acts 17:11) to find out just what the blood has accomplished for us.

The Search

We need to find out what we have through the blood of Jesus Christ. We then can be assured that the things revealed by Scripture are the *"better things"* for our benefit. In other words, the search for these truths should enable us to say, "We have _____ through, or because of, the shed blood of Jesus Christ." Our search will enable us to fill in the blank.

For example, a Scripture just mentioned tells us we have redemption through the precious blood of Christ (1 Peter 1:18-19). So we can say, "We have redemption through the blood of Jesus." When we believe this and make it a part of our testimony, two things happen. First, we set ourselves in agreement with what the blood of Jesus has accomplished. We can be sure that one of the *"better things"* the blood is speaking is that it provided our redemption for salvation. We *"submit ourselves to God"* in this way. Secondly, we *"resist the devil"* by saying to him, "I am redeemed by the blood of Jesus."

Is this academic? Just a play on words? No, it is real, and it is serious. A key verse is:

[11]They [Christians] *overcame him* [the devil] *by the blood of the Lamb, and by the word of their testimony.*

(Revelation 12:11)

"The word of our testimony" needs to include what the blood of Jesus Christ has accomplished for us. I therefore believe the next chapter on the blood's benefits for us needs to be diligently studied and incorporated into our understanding of spiritual realities.

We can overcome the devil when we know and agree with what the blood has accomplished. It is speaking of divine accomplishments. We need to speak of them also.

We add the speaking blood to the spiritual tug-of-war going on all around us. That makes "Five against one—no contest!"

Chapter 15

Benefits through Jesus' Blood

I n this chapter we will outline the many benefits God has provided for us through the blood of Jesus Christ. These benefits range from our salvation to our complete restored fellowship with the Father.

In a search of New Testament Scriptures explicitly linking the blood of Jesus Christ with a benefit for us, I have found more than twelve different topics. In addition, there are many topics where the blood of Jesus is only implicitly mentioned. An excellent example of this is, *"by whose stripes ye were healed"* (1 Peter 2:24). In this case it is obvious that the blood of Jesus was shed when he was scourged at the cruel whipping post for us. Our benefit in this case? *"Ye were healed!"*

Let us consider these marvelous benefits. Although we present them separately, they do not represent separate spiritual experiences. The blood of Jesus has within it all the benefits purchased at the cross for us. Let us see what Scripture says about the precious blood of Jesus Christ.

Redemption

REDEMPTION: *deliverance from sin; salvation.*

Redemption points to a price paid, a cost. W. E. Vine (1966, p. 263) states that the word redemption means "especially of purchasing a slave with a view to his freedom." Redemption would be the word to describe a wealthy man buying slaves at an auction and then setting them free.

Every human being is born into the devil's kingdom of darkness (Colossians 1:13). Our redemption from this slavery was purchased at a great cost. The amount? It is immeasurable. It was the blood of Jesus Christ.

A moment's imagination could generate several other ways that God could have redeemed man. Consider money as one example. Remember the money in the mouth of the fish (Matthew 17:27)? Remember, *"The silver is mine, and the gold is mine, saith the Lord"* (Haggai 2:8)? No, God did not use money. He used the shed blood of Jesus Christ to redeem men.

Consider these verses:

*⁷We have redemption through his blood.
(Ephesians 1:7, Colossians 1:14)*

*¹²By his own blood he entered in once into
the holy place, having obtained eternal
redemption for us.   (Hebrews 9:12)*

*¹⁸You were not redeemed with corruptible
things...
¹⁹But with the precious blood of Christ.
(1 Peter 1:18-19)*

*⁹Thou...hast redeemed us to God by thy
blood.   (Revelation 5:9)*

Look at one result of being redeemed. We
are made *"kings and priests and we shall reign
on the earth"* (Revelation 5:10). How? By the
blood!

Forgiveness of Sins

FORGIVENESS: *the act of forgiving;
the state of being forgiven; disposition
or willingness to forgive.*

SIN: *transgression of divine law.*

"Who can forgive sins but God only?" (Mark 2:7). And **how** does God forgive sins? He forgives by the blood of Jesus as stated in the Scriptures:

[7]We have redemption through his blood, the forgiveness of sins.   (Ephesians 1:7)

[22]Without the shedding of blood there is no forgiveness.   (Hebrews 9:22 NIV)

God's way for forgiveness of sins is by the blood of Jesus.

Cleansing

CLEANSE: *to make clean, to purge, to purify.*

The cleansing of sins by the blood is best known from this Scripture in First John:

[7]The blood of Jesus Christ his Son cleanseth us from all sin.
[9]If we confess our sins, he is faithful and just to forgive us our sins, and to cleanse us from all unrighteousness [by His blood].   (1 John 1:7,9)

Other Scriptures also reveal cleansing by the blood:

174

*14The blood of Christ..purge [cleanse] your
conscience from dead works to serve the
living God.* (Hebrews 9:14)
*5Unto him that loved us, and washed
[cleansed] us from our sins in his own
blood.* (Revelation 1:5)

How are we forgiven and cleansed? By the
blood of Jesus Christ!

There are differences in being redeemed
and forgiven and cleansed. Suppose a man
accidentally backs his car over a small child,
killing him. He is obviously guilty and is sen-
tenced to prison. Later he is released on parole
(redeemed). In a legal sense, that act has
satisfied the law. Next, the family of the child
come to him and forgive him. That act removes
external guilt feelings in relationship with
others. Even though the man has been redeemed and forgiven, there remain internal
memories that need to be dealt with. The
traumatic experience etched in the man's
memories as sin needs **cleansing.**

Likewise with each one of us, if the blood
just redeemed us, we would legally be set free
from Satan's kingdom, but we would still not
be completely restored to perfect fellowship
with God the Father. Then, too, if the blood
only redeemed us and forgave our sins, we still
would not be completely restored to perfect
fellowship with God the Father. An internal

cleansing needs to take place. But, praise God, the Word also says that the blood also cleanses us.

Justification

JUSTIFICATION: *the act of God whereby man is absolved of guilt for sin.*

Absolved of guilt means acquittal! Discharge! Freedom! Not guilty! By nature, man is not only a child of the evil one, but also a transgressor and a criminal. By nature, we were under a verdict of "guilty." In redemption, man receives a new life and a new nature; in justification, a new standing. God declares righteous (justifies) the person who believes on Christ. By believing, we are given a verdict of "acquittal."

How are we justified? Martin Luther asked a similar question. Out of his answer came the very foundation for the Protestant Reformation. *"Justification by faith"* (Romans 5:1) is the bottom line. He could have said, *"justification by blood"* (Romans 5:9).

These passages speak of *"being justified by faith"* and *"being justified by his blood"* in the same context. As I meditated on these passages, the Holy Spirit showed me it was not an either/or situation. That is, we were not either *"justified by faith"* or *"justified by his blood,"* but we were *"justified by faith in his blood."* It is clear that the object of one's faith is the blood of Jesus Christ in these verses. Hence, Martin Luther's bottom line could well have been, "Justification by faith in the blood of Jesus Christ."

In Romans 5:9, Weymouth actually uses the word *"acquitted"* instead of *"justified"*: *"Much more, then, now that we have been acquitted by His blood..."* God declares us *"acquitted"*! Why? How? Because of the blood of Jesus Christ.

Reconciliation

RECONCILIATION: *an act of reconciling; the state of being reconciled; the process of making consistent or compatible.*

The Twentieth Century New Testament (TCNT) translation states:

[25]*For God set him before the world, to be, by the shedding of His blood, a means of reconciliation through faith.*

(Romans 3:25)

The important clause, *"by the shedding of his blood,"* reveals how reconciliation between God and man is accomplished. Thus, another benefit of the blood is to be reconciled with Almighty God.

The King James rendering of Romans 3:25 uses the word *"propitiation."* Simply stated, to propitiate is to appease. An opposite meaning is wrath. A fuller definition of propitiation means "the removal of divine wrath by God offering His Son." *"By the shedding of his blood,"* the divine wrath towards sin is propitiated, and, as a consequence of this propitiation, the punishment due to sin is not inflicted upon us. Let's go one more step. This noninfliction of penalty is forgiveness. Forgiveness, in turn, leads to reconciliation. Whew! All of that for the one word *"propitiate."*

Scriptures have much to say about the wrath of God. It seems that the New Testament represents Christ's death (His shed blood) as propitiating God's holy wrath against sin. As Romans 3:25 (TCNT) begins, *"For God set him before the world"* brings out the wonderful, wonderful fact that God took the initiative in reconciliation. We respond *"through faith in his blood"* as in the same verse in the King James Version.

In the Scriptures, reconciliation is applied to both God and man. (See Romans 5:10 and 11

Corinthians 5:18-20.) The meaning is something like this:

> At first God and man stood face to face with each other. In sinning, Adam turned his back upon God. Then God turned His back on Adam. Christ's death has satisfied the demands of God and now God has again turned His face toward man. It remains for man to turn round about and face God. Since God has been reconciled by the death of His Son, man is now entreated to be reconciled to God.
>
> (Thiessen 1949, p. 327)

For those of us who like formulas, here is one to meditate on:

BLOOD + FAITH = RECONCILIATION

Another Scripture says it this way:

> *[20]Through him to reconcile to himself all things...by making peace through his blood, shed on the cross.*
>
> *(Colossians 1:20 NIV)*

Sanctification

Sanctification: *to make holy; consecrate; to purify or free from sin.*

I use a companion Scripture to the well known verse, *"Without faith it is impossible to please God "* (Hebrews 11:6). It is:

> [14]*Follow peace with all men, and holiness, without which no man shall see the Lord.*
> *(Hebrews 12:14)*

I reword it to say, "Without holiness no man shall see the Lord." I also keep in mind that the same Greek word translated holiness is also translated sanctification.

I want to please God (faith), and I want to see the Lord (holiness). Faith and sanctification are the keys to doing so.

Sanctification (holiness) needs to be preached and taught much more in the church. May this treatise present the basis for preaching and teaching sanctification, that is, the blood of Jesus Christ.

We can do nothing to sanctify ourselves. However, there are definite means we may employ in our sanctification. First, faith in Jesus is required. He who believes in Christ is sanctified **positionally** by His blood. Jesus *"is made unto us [Christians] sanctification"* (1 Corinthians 1:30). Second must come the **pursuit** after holiness. This is a process extending throughout life. Third, God has already set apart to Himself every one who believes in Christ; now the believer is to set himself apart to God for His use. This entails a definite **surrender** of our lives to God.

Does the Word link sanctification and the blood of Jesus Christ? Hebrews explicitly does so:

> [29]The blood of the covenant that sanctified him. *(Hebrews 10:29 NIV)*
> [12]Jesus also suffered...to make the people holy [sanctified] through his own blood. *(Hebrews 13:12 NIV)*

How are we made holy **positionally?** *"Through his own blood."* What is the basis for a lifetime **pursuit** of holiness? *"Through his own blood."* On what ground can we make a definite **surrender** of our lives to God? *"Through his own blood."* Holiness, that we may *"see the Lord,"* is a marvelous benefit of the shed blood.

Several implicit references linking our sanctification and the blood of Jesus Christ are also in Hebrews:

> [10]We are sanctified through the offering of the body of Jesus Christ once for all. *(Hebrews 10:10)*
> [14]For by one offering he hath perfected for ever them that are sanctified. *(Hebrews 10:14)*

Holiness is perhaps the most difficult benefit of the blood for Christians to appropriate. The devil hates holiness in a child of God. He attacks the believer along this line most vehemently. In addition, the lack of preaching and teaching of holiness weakens the believer's knowledge of this truth.

I believe each one of the benefits presented in this chapter is important in itself. As mentioned above, the blood has accomplished so much that more than ten explicit benefits that are given in Scripture. Let us go on to find out what more God has done for us through the blood of Jesus Christ.

Peace

PEACE: *cessation of or freedom from any strife or dissension.*

One of my favorite Bible prayers is Colossians 1:9-22. Verse two plainly states that Paul was writing to Christians, *"to the saints and faithful brethren in Christ which are at Colosse."* To make the prayer more personal, I substitute my name and city in verse two. Note that verse 14 contains the benefits of redemption and forgiveness through His blood as described earlier. Then notice Paul's prayer comes to a close with another benefit:

²⁰And, having made peace through the blood of his cross, by him to reconcile all things unto himself; by him, I say, whether they be things in earth, or things in heaven.   *(Colossians 1:20)*

We have peace with God *"through the blood of his cross."* Read on in verse 20. What is the result of Jesus making peace through His blood? It was *"to reconcile all things unto himself."* So here is another reference to the blood of Jesus in reconciling God and the human race. Actually, because of the phrase, *"things in earth, or things in heaven"* in the same verse, the peace and therefore the reconciliation are universal in application. That is, God has reconciled to Himself not only man, but also things in heaven. Now that is something to meditate about!

I find it very interesting that the verses between the first and second statements of the benefits of His blood, that is, verses 15 through 19, are some of the most powerful statements about Jesus Christ in all of the Bible. Couple these verses with others such as *"the Lamb slain from the foundation of the world"* (Revelation 13:8), and you see why we cannot separate Jesus and His shed blood.

Our peace with God is based on the shed blood of Jesus Christ.

Approach to God

APPROACH: *to come near or nearer to; to come near to in quality, character, time, or condition.*

GOD: *the Supreme Being, the creator and ruler of the universe.*

How can man approach God? This is one of the most fundamental questions that we can ask.

Some say that God doesn't exist so their answer is simply not to ask the question! Others say that God may exist but it is impossible to know anything about Him. Their answer is a simple, "We can't approach God." Still others answer, "We can approach God but we don't know exactly how." This answer has generated all kinds of religions all around the world.

Then one day Jesus Himself answered the question very simply:

> [6]*I am the way, the truth, and the life: no man cometh unto the Father, but by me.*
> *(John 14:6)*

Let us make the question personal: "How can I approach God?" Jesus said, *"By me."* Thank you. We accept that. In line with the

theme of this book, we would ask an additiona
question: "Jesus, what is it about You tha
permits us to approach God?"

Let me elaborate a little further. "Jesus, is
it Your virgin birth that allows me to approach
God? Or is it the miracles You performed? On
is it Your sinless life?"

I imagine Him answering me, "The answer
is 'yes' to all your questions, Bob. But all
these and more culminate in a single answer
which you can find in Hebrews." Looking up
His written answer, I read:

> [19]*Having therefore, brethren, boldness to
> enter into the holiest by the blood of Jesus.*
> *(Hebrews 10:19)*

"*By the blood of Jesus.*" That is my answer!
The blood is my approach to God! Notice the
word, "*brethren.*" That means Christians.
Notice the first word, "*Having.*" That means we
have something as Christians. What is it?
"*Boldness*" or "*confidence.*" That means we have
boldness as Christians. Boldness for what? "*To
enter into the holiest.*" That is, to approach God
the Father in His very presence. And, again,
what is our boldness based on? Remember,
several Old Testament men were bold in themselves to touch the ark containing God's Presence and they were immediately struck dead.

What is the basis of our boldness to approach God? *"By the blood of Jesus!"*

A companion verse to this is:

> [16]*Let us come boldly unto the throne of grace, that we may obtain mercy, and find grace to help in time of need.*
>
> (Hebrews 4:16)

Who? *"Us."* How? *"Boldly."* Where? *"Unto the throne."* Why? *"That we may obtain mercy, and find grace to help in time of need."* What is the basis for doing so? *"The blood of Jesus!"*

Another statement of this truth is:

> [13]*Now in Christ Jesus you who were once faraway have been brought near through the blood of Christ.*
>
> (Ephesians 2:13 NIV)

How can man approach God? The answer is, *"in Christ Jesus...through the blood of Christ."*

I use this benefit daily. I pray to God the Father in the name of Jesus. And I also recognize that my approach into His Presence is by the blood of Jesus.

Our approach to God the Father is by the blood of God the Son.

Eternal Inheritance

ETERNAL: *lasting forever; without beginning or end; always existing; perpetual; ceaseless; endless; not subject to change.*

INHERITANCE: *to take or receive (property, a right, a title, etc.) by succession or will, as an heir.*

The blood of Jesus Christ has also provided the wonderful benefit of an eternal inheritance for us. So that we don't take this lightly, recall that the alternative is *"everlasting punishment"* (Matthew 25:46).

We find in Hebrews that Jesus:

> *[12]By his own blood entered in once into the holy place, having obtained eternal redemption for us.* (Hebrews 9:12)

As we saw in the section on redemption, this verse is one that helps to establish the fact that our redemption is by His blood. Recall that the word translated *"redemption"* includes the meaning of purchasing slaves at an auction and then setting them free. I want to show something one step further. It is well and good that a slave be redeemed and then set free by his purchaser. It is something much better if the freed slave is then adopted as a son by the purchaser to share in his inheritance!

Does the Word link the blood of Jesus with our inheritance? It certainly is implied in many Scriptures, and I believe by careful study it is explicitly stated in the context of the following:

> [12]*Neither by the blood of goats and calves, but by his own blood he entered in once into the holy place, having obtained eternal redemption for us.*
> [13]*For if the blood of bulls and of goats, and the ashes of an heifer sprinkling the unclean, sanctifieth to the purifying of the flesh;*
> [14]*How much more shall the blood of Christ, who through the eternal Spirit offered himself without spot to God, purge your conscience from dead works to serve the living God?*
> [15]*And for this cause he is the mediator of the new testament, that by means of death, for the redemption of the transgressions that were under the first. testament, they which are called might receive the promise of eternal inheritance.* (Hebrews 9:12-15)

Verse 15 ends with "*they which are called might receiveth the promise of eternal inheritance.*" First of all, "*they which are called*" are the same "*holy brethren partakers of the heavenly calling*" of Hebrews 3:1. That is, the author is definitely writing to Christians. Secondly, *"the promise of eternal inheritance"* has been purchased for them. How? By *"his own blood"* of verse 12 which is referred to as *"by means of death"* in verse 15. This section of Scripture is talking about the sacrifice of Christ which established the new covenant. The sacrifice of Christ is synonymous with shedding His blood on our behalf.

Let me sketch this development as:

> *Christ...by His own blood...obtained eternal redemption for us...that we might receive the promise of eternal inheritance.*

By the blood, we are redeemed **and** we are promised an eternal inheritance!

We skipped over verse 14 regarding the purging benefit of the blood of Christ. Let us consider this next.

Purging

PURGING: *to rid of whatever is impure or undesirable; to become cleansed or purified.*

A purging action by the blood of Jesus is presented in Hebrews 9:14:

¹⁴*How much more shall the blood of
Christ, who through the eternal Spirit
offered himself without spot to God, purge
your conscience from dead works to serve
the living God?* (Hebrews 9:14)

This verse is very potent. It is one of the
few verses in the entire Bible which present
God as a triune Being—Father, Son, and Holy
Spirit. Their modifiers are revealing—*"blood of
Christ," "eternal Spirit,"* and *"living God."* The
subject of the verse is the blood, the verb is
purge, and the object is our conscience (us).
The relationship of the Trinity, the blood, the
purging, and us in the same verse is that we
may serve the living God. This is indeed a very
remarkable verse!

The phrase *"purge your conscience from
dead works"* needs to be elaborated upon. I find
it quite unexpected. Let me explain. Re-read
the above verse with a blank space in place of
the phrase *"purge your conscience from dead
works."* Now ask yourself the question, "What
should be inserted in the blank space?" Or,
"What is the blood of Jesus going to do in order
that we may *'serve the living God'?*" Start
filling in the blank space with your answers.
This is a very interesting exercise—try it on
someone and see what answers they come up
with.

My process went like this. After some meditation, I came up with the truth that if I am *"to serve the living God"* then the blood of Christ will have to make me pure and clean. Yes, the blood is for cleansing as we showed earlier. In this verse, the synonymous word *"purge"* is used. It reads *"purge your,"* so it is speaking to me directly; it is speaking of my conscience. So now the blank space has been partially filled with *"purge your...."* Now comes the unexpected part. Ask another question like, **"What** is the blood of Christ going to purge in me that I may serve the living God?" We already know the blood cleanses from sins and unrighteousness as pointed out earlier. What else needs cleansing or purging? Giving up and reading verse 14 for the answer, I see that the blood needs to purge my conscience. From what? *"Dead works."* Why? So that I may *"serve the living God."*

What is our conscience? A dictionary definition is:

CONSCIENCE: *the sense of what is right or wrong in one's conduct or motives impelling one toward right action; the ethical and moral principles that control or inhibit the actions or thoughts of an individual.*

191

I notice that the first definition urges us toward right action and the second keeps us from wrong action. In any case, I think of conscience as a policeman within us, enforcing the law so to speak. Conscience discriminates between right and wrong based on a standard. It also is impulsive, urging us to take action or refrain from action based on that standard. In other words, conscience judges according to the standard given it.

Conscience is undeveloped in the infant. It is imperfectly developed in the adult. Scriptures teach that conscience may be *"defiled"* (1 Corinthians 8:7) and *"seared"* (1 Timothy 4:2). So if the moral and ethical standard accepted by the individual is imperfect, the decisions of conscience will be imperfect.

Conscience is uniform and infallible, in the sense that it always decides rightly according to the law given it. Saul before his conversion is a familiar example.

The only true standard for conscience is the Word of God as interpreted by the Holy Spirit. With this understanding of what our conscience is, the phrase *"purge your conscience from dead works"* is much more understandable. Taken in context, the *"dead works"* refer to the keeping of the Old Testament law. The book of Hebrews was addressed to Jewish Christians who evidently were continuing to practice their animal sacrifices rather than accepting God's provision of the sacrifice of Jesus Christ and receiving the benefits of His blood.

Applied to us today, the *"dead works"* include worshiping God according to man's rules and regulations. An obvious example, taken from the theme of this book, is practicing a "bloodless religion." That is, the worship of God without any reference to the shed blood of Jesus Christ would be *"dead works."* The fact of the matter is that we worship God according to the standard built into our consciences since we were born. If the development of our consciences has not been built on the standard of the Word of God, then our consciences are *"defiled."* Other examples of dead works are listed in Galatians 5:19-21 where the phrase *"works of the flesh"* could have been stated *"[dead] works of the flesh."*

Our text verse gives the remedy. It says to *"purge your conscience from dead works."* What is going to do the purging? *"The blood of Christ."* What is going to receive the purging? Our conscience. Who must allow the purging? We must.

Three final points are relevant: First, *"Be not conformed to this world; but be ye transformed by the renewing of your mind"* (Romans 12:2). Second, renewing also comes from the blood of Christ *"purging our consciences from dead works"* (Hebrews 9:14). Third, why should we submit ourselves to this purging process? *"To serve the living God"* (Hebrews 9:14). I combine these three points like this:

> Be not conformed to dead works; but allow the blood of Jesus to renew your mind and purge your conscience to serve God.

Sprinkled

SPRINKLED: *to scatter (a liquid, powder, etc.) in drops or particles; to disperse or distribute here and there.*

I now introduce a benefit of the blood of Jesus which I have never heard preached or taught. It is the topic of sprinkled blood. Consider the following verse:

> *²⁴The sprinkled blood that speaks a better word than the blood of Abel.*
> *(Hebrews 12:24 NIV)*

We used this verse before when discovering that the blood of Jesus is a speaking blood. The same verse states Jesus' blood is also a sprinkled blood.

Peter introduces his first letter with the concept of sprinkled blood:

¹Peter, an apostle of Jesus Christ, to the...
²Elect...through sanctification of the spirit
unto obedience and sprinkling of the blood
of Jesus Christ.   *(1 Peter 1:1-2)*

Peter, writing to Christians, mentions three things in his salutation: sanctification, obedience, and sprinkling of the blood. The last two items are brought out very clearly in Moffat's translation:

²To obey Jesus Christ and be sprinkled
with his blood.   *(1 Peter 1:2)*

Christians were greeted with instructions *"to obey Jesus Christ and be sprinkled with His blood."* What makes this Scripture so exciting is that it is broken up into two distinct parts of obedience and sprinkling. We have no trouble understanding the meaning of obeying Jesus Christ. However, what is the meaning of being sprinkled with the blood of Jesus Christ?

Five insights arise about the topic of sprinkled blood:

1. Peter wrote his letter some thirty years after Jesus was crucified, buried, and raised again. Thirty years later, he tells Christians to obey Jesus Christ. We have no problem understanding that. Also thirty years later,

he tells Christians to be sprinkled with the blood of Jesus Christ! We may not understand that. However, this is certainly another proof that the blood is still living if Christians could be sprinkled with it thirty years after it was shed at Calvary. Also, Christians were instructed to be sprinkled with the blood as something to do on purpose.

2. An Old Testament counterpart of people being sprinkled with blood is concisely reviewed in Hebrews 9:19. At the ceremony where the Old Testament was ratified, *"Moses...took the blood of calves and of goats...and sprinkled both the book and all the people."* Sprinkling of blood is found in both the Old and New Testaments.

3. The *"blood of sprinkling"* of Hebrews 12:24 and *"having our hearts sprinkled"* in Hebrews 10:22 are other examples of sprinkled blood.

4. A few years ago, I read of a traveling woman evangelist who ministered in the early part of this century. I recall that she sprinkled the audience with the blood of Jesus as she came out to minister in her meetings. This sprinkling was done spiritually; real blood was not used, of course. The

response was oftentimes met with people rushing to the altar to get saved, to confess their sins, and such (Woodworth-Etter, pp. 251-256).

5. A rite in the Roman Catholic Church is still performed today where the priest uses a motion of sprinkling the people. I believe the basis of that action could be 1 Peter 1:2 where the believers were admonished to be sprinkled with the blood of Jesus Christ.

My wife and I have ministered by sprinkling the blood of Jesus on people who came forward in our meetings. We have received many testimonies of people being helped by this form of ministry.

We know we should obey Jesus Christ. Let us act on the second part of that verse and also be sprinkled with His blood!

Healing

HEAL: *to make whole or sound; to restore to health; to free from ailment.*

All of the topics presented in this chapter are benefits linked explicitly to the blood of Jesus Christ as revealed in the New Testament. I could end the chapter at this point.

However, a very important benefit provided by the blood would be omitted if I did so. It is the healing of our physical bodies. Healing is a benefit provided by the shed blood.

> [13]*The body...is for the Lord and the Lord is for the body.* (1 Corinthians 6:13)
> [19]*Know ye not that your body is a temple of the Holy Ghost which is in you?*
> (1 Corinthians 6:19)

As Christians, our bodies are inhabited by the Holy Spirit. Our bodies are for the Lord, and we are assured that *"the Lord is for the body."* Notice it does not say, "The Lord is against the body," or even, "The Lord is neutral about the body." The Lord is for the body.

The Lord being for the body is further amplified by the marvelous Scripture:

> [31]*If God be for us, who can be against us?*
> (Romans 8:31)

Once we realize that the Lord is for the body, we will yield to His benefit of healing provided by the blood of Jesus.

Did Jesus ever say that He would provide healing for us? Yes, He did—in the same breath, so to speak, when He also said He would provide salvation for us. The occasion? The Lord's Supper. The time? The night before

He was crucified. The place? The Upper Room. The words? *"Take, eat: this is my body which is broken for you"* (1 Corinthians 11:24), and *"This cup is the new testament in my blood, which is shed for you"* (Luke 22:20).

Jesus announced that His body would be broken for us (physical healing) and that His blood would be shed for us (spiritual blessings).

Let us consider a familiar Scripture to illustrate a benefit of the blood of Jesus is our physical healing:

> [24]*Who his own self bare our sins in his own body on the tree that we being dead to sins should live unto righteousness; by whose stripes ye were healed.*
>
> *(1 Peter 2:24)*

The first thing I notice about this Scripture is that it speaks of Jesus bearing our sins and our sicknesses. Let's look at the last phrase in four different translations:

> *By whose stripes ye were healed.*   *(KJV)*
>
> *His bruising was your healing.*   *(TCNT)*
>
> *By his wounds you have been healed.*
>   *(NEB)*
>
> *It was the suffering that he bore which has healed you.*   *(PHILLIPS)*

Seven very powerful truths are contained in this one short phrase:

1. The **benefactor** is the man Jesus. An angel or another spirit being could not shed blood for us.

2. The **recipient** is the Christian. Jesus didn't die for the fallen angels or for animals. He didn't die just for His own people, the Old Testament Jews. He died for *"whoever believes."* Jesus actually died for me and for you.

3. The **means** was Jesus' *"stripes," "bruising," "wounds," "suffering."* The means was not spiritual. It was not an easy, trivial thing for God to do. The means of Jesus' death was not by just a verbal decree of God saying something like, "Because of Jesus' perfect life, your sins are forgiven." He voluntarily gave up His life. He really did bleed and suffer. He was tortured to death while He suffered beatings, thorns, and nakedness.

4. The **benefit** is our healing—healing for cancer, healing for heart trouble, healing for every type of disease. *"Himself took our infirmities, and bare our sicknesses"* (Matthew 8:17). Upon believing and acting on this benefit of the blood of Jesus, people are really

healed, just in the same way people are really born again.

5. The **time** is past tense—*"were,"* *"was,"* *"have been,"* *"has."* It is the same time our redemption, justification, and reconciliation were provided—at the cross nearly 2000 years ago. It isn't correct to say that Jesus is going to heal us. He has healed us. Let's not put the time of our healing in the future when we get to heaven. The Lord is for our bodies, now.

6. The shed **blood** of Jesus Christ is not mentioned, but it is certainly implied. The Word says Jesus suffered scourging. This certainly spilled his blood.

7. Therefore, **our physical healing** is included in the benefits provided by the shed blood of Jesus Christ.

Yes, healing for our physical bodies is one of the benefits of the shed blood of Jesus Christ. Let us appropriate it into our lives. Do not spiritualize it. Jesus came to deliver us from our sins and sicknesses. The very word *"salvation"* sums up all the blessings bestowed by God on men in Christ through the Holy Spirit. Thank you, Father God, for providing healing for our bodies through the blood of Jesus Christ.

Speaking Blood

The blood of Jesus is alive. It is speaking. It is speaking *"better things"* than that of Abel's blood. I have shown it is speaking of divine accomplishments for our benefit. The above topics which link the blood to a benefit are the kinds of things the blood is undoubtedly speaking. The blood is speaking for us; we, in turn, need to speak our faith about the blood.

Chapter 16

Plead The Blood

And they overcame him by the blood of the lamb and by the word of their testimony; and they loved not their lives unto the death.
—Revelation 12:11

We are now ready to more fully answer the question, "What does it mean to 'plead the blood of Jesus Christ'?"

We have seen how God revealed to Paul that the death and shed blood of Jesus Christ is *"of first importance."* Then we saw that His shed blood is a "speaking blood" and is active today for our benefit. Next, we gave many examples of what the blood of Jesus Christ has provided for us and therefore what the blood is undoubtedly saying.

Now, let us see what it means for us to "plead the blood." It is one thing for the blood to speak for us. It is another thing for us to "plead the blood." We are passive in the first case. But, when we are active in "pleading the blood," a whole new dimension of spiritual power opens to us.

Many examples of "pleading the blood" are given by H.A. Maxwell Whyte in his book, *The Power of the Blood*. I include one here as an illustration:

> "Pastor Whyte, will you pray for my eyes?" Betty asked me one day. She was a young girl of sixteen who worked in a Fish N' Chips store in Toronto.
>
> "Why, certainly, Betty," I replied. "Let's just believe God together and plead the Blood of Jesus." I looked at her for a moment and felt the great compassion of Jesus stirring within me. She was totally blind in her right eye, and her left eye was wandering so that it was very difficult for her to focus at all. She was wearing very, very thick glasses—the thickest she could get.
>
> I began to pray for her, pleading the Blood strongly and emphatically. Instantly, the Lord restored the sight of her right eye.
>
> "Oh, praise the Lord!" she squealed. "I can see!" We rejoiced together at the mercy of the Lord.
>
> Over a period of weeks, the wandering eye began to focus and in a matter of months, she had 20-20 vision. That was twenty years ago, and she is still healed.
>
> This is but one example of hundreds upon hundreds of stories which I could relate, demonstrating the power of the blood of Jesus."
>
> (Whyte 1973, pp. 11-12)

Appeal Earnestly

The word *"plead"* is found many times in the Old Testament but not once in the New Testament! The dictionary definitions are:

PLEAD: *to appeal or entreat earnestly; to use arguments or persuasions for or against something.*

The definitions of "appeal earnestly" and to "to use arguments for or against something" witness with my spirit what I am trying to demonstrate.

The Passover

Let's use the phrase "appeal earnestly" as a synonym for "plead." What Biblical account would illustrate the definition to "appeal earnestly" the blood? I believe the best example from the Old Testament is the Exodus from Egypt. I want to center in on the Passover account when some 2.5 million Israelites walked out on 430 years of slavery in Egypt under the leadership of Moses and by the miracles of God. The pertinent passage is found in Exodus:

⁴And Moses said, Thus saith the Lord, About midnight will I go out into the midst of Egypt:

⁵And all the firstborn in the land of Egypt shall die...

¹And the Lord spake unto Moses and Aaron in the land of Egypt, saying,

³...take to them every man a lamb...a lamb for a house:

⁶...and the whole assembly of the congregation of Israel shall kill it in the evening.

⁷And they shall take of the blood, and strike it on the two side posts and on the upper door post of the houses, wherein they shall eat it.

¹³And the blood shall be to you for a token [sign NIV] upon the houses where ye are: and when I see the blood, I will pass over you, and the plague shall not be upon you to destroy you, when I smite the land of Egypt.

²¹Then Moses called for all the elders of Israel and said unto them, Draw out and take you a lamb according to your families, and kill the passover.

²²And ye shall take a bunch of hyssop, and dip it in the blood that is in the basin, and strike the lintel and the two side posts with the blood that is in the basin; and none of you shall go out at the door of his house until the morning.

²³For the Lord will pass through to smite the Egyptians; and when he seeth the

blood upon the lintel, and on the two side
posts, the Lord will pass over the door, and
will not suffer the destroyer to come in
unto your houses to smite you.
(Exodus 11:4-5; 12:1, 3, 6-7, 13, 21-23)

God spoke to Moses, and Moses, in turn, spoke to the people the condition for their deliverance. The last of the plagues against Pharaoh was to be the death of the firstborn. The Israelites would escape this terrible plague if they applied the blood to the lintel and the two door posts as instructed. If the blood was not applied, death surely came:

[30]And Pharaoh rose up in the night, he,
and all his servants, and all the Egyp-
tians; and there was a great cry in Egypt;
for there was not a house where there was
not one dead.   (Exodus 12:30)

Two fundamental facts are evident in this example of "appealing earnestly" the blood.

First, if the God-given instructions were not followed, death came. Both the basin containing the blood and the hyssop (a mint plant of the Middle East) could be sitting on the table. Having the blood available and the means to sprinkle it would not be enough. The instructions were to dip the hyssop in the basin of blood and sprinkle the lintel and doorposts.

Let me bring the analogy closer to home. The blood of Jesus Christ has been shed. It is available for every Christian to use. Our mouths correspond to the hyssop. It is available for use. We must bring the two together to overcome the devil in his accusations against us. Is this analogy scriptural? Consider the following:

> *⁹The great dragon...that old serpent, called the Devil, and Satan, which deceiveth the whole world,*
> *¹¹And they overcame him by the blood of the Lamb, and by the word of their testimony.* (Revelation 12:9,11)

How do we as Christians overcome the devil? The God-given provisions are revealed by this verse. They are the blood of Jesus and the word of our testimony concerning His blood. The blood of Jesus has been shed. It is in the basin, so to speak. The word of our testimony is within us. It corresponds to the hyssop, so to speak. What do we do? Do nothing and be overcome by the devil? Or, use the blood and our testimony regarding it and thereby overcome the devil? The analogy is clear. Jesus, the Lamb of God, has shed His blood for us. The benefits of that blood were outlined in Chapter 15. We overcome the devil *"by the blood of the*

Lamb, and by the word of their [our] testimony" concerning what the blood has done for us.

A second fundamental fact concerning "appealing earnestly" the blood of Jesus is also evident. After the Israelite followed God's instructions and sprinkled the blood on the lintel and doorposts, he stayed inside his house the rest of the night. What did he do during this time? We can be sure he and his family didn't sleep!

> *[30]There was a great cry in Egypt; for there was not a house where there was not one dead.*   *(Exodus 12:30)*

A great cry is God's description of that horrible event. Surely the Israelites understood what was happening. Again, what did they do during that night? I most certainly believe they "pleaded the blood." Or, they "appealed earnestly the blood." Or, they "used arguments for or against something" in relation to the blood applied to their doorways.

I imagine the Israelites inside their house were huddled around their firstborn and were loudly crying out to God that they had followed His instructions. They "pleaded the blood." They "appealed earnestly the blood." They cried out using the argument that they had sprinkled the blood as they were instructed. The

Israelites rested their case on the sprinkled blood.

Again, the analogy is clear for us. We are to "plead the blood" for our deliverance. We are to overcome the devil by pleading the blood of Jesus Christ and by our word of testimony regarding its power to deliver us. We rest our case on the shed blood of Jesus Christ.

During the night of the Passover in Egypt, the Israelites were spared the death of their firstborn by following God's instructions given through Moses. Their faith was centered on correctly following the instructions. Naturally, when the hour of tempest came, I imagine they pleaded their case before God, "appealing earnestly" and "using arguments" that they had carried out His instructions correctly.

In the same way, when we are threatened to be overcome by the devil's attacks, we can plead that the blood of Jesus Christ avails for us. We may not understand how it works anymore than the Israelites could understand how blood on the doorpost would prevent the death of their firstborn. But we, like them, are overcomers by "pleading the blood."

A New Song

Let's next consider an example from the New Testament. The power of the blood of

Jesus is very evident in a brief passage in the fifth chapter of Revelation. In this scene in heaven, the four beasts and the 24 elders worship and sing a new song to our Lord as He takes a book out of the hand of God on the throne. What are the words that are sung to Jesus? If you have not read the scriptural account yet, it may be instructive to pause and think of what would be sung to Him. Will the words of the new song deal with God's creation? With angels? With miracles? No, the song glorifies Jesus and His shed blood that redeemed us thereby making us kings and priests to rule on earth! The new song links Jesus, His blood, and us together! Here it is:

> [9]*Thou art worthy to take the book, and to open the seals thereof: for thou wast slain, and hast redeemed us to God by thy blood out of every kindred, and tongue, and people, and nation;*
> [10]*And hast made us unto our God kings and priests: and we shall reign on the earth.* (Revelation 5:9-10)

Notice Jesus was slain. Why? To redeem us to God! Who? Every kindred and tongue and people and nation! How? By His blood! What? We are made unto our God kings and priests. Where? We shall reign on the earth!

The next time the devil challenges your salvation, sing this new song to him. We are redeemed by the blood of Jesus Christ. Our testimony to this fact overcomes the devil. Our answer to the devil rests on the blood of the Lamb and our testimony regarding it. In fact, this particular verse doesn't stop with our redemption by His blood. Notice that it goes on to say the blood *"has made us unto our God kings and priests"*! Then, for the knockout blow, tell the devil that *"we shall reign on the earth"* because of the shed blood of Jesus Christ. In other words, we will soon be replacing the devil —*"the god of this world"* (11 Corinthians 4:4)— as rulers of this world!

We Add Our Testimony

We know that Jesus and the Holy Spirit intercede for us. We know that angels minister for us. We have learned that the blood speaks for us. All this activity is working for our behalf. Now, let us add our testimony.

Let us continually "plead the blood" of Jesus Christ by adding our testimony of the power of His blood for redemption, forgiveness of sins, cleansing, and all the other benefits we have received. Let us voice this testimony out loud. Let us add the words of our testimony of the power of the blood to the heavenly chorus all around us. Let us "plead the blood"!

Chapter 17

Our Speaking Faith

*It is written: "I believed; therefore I have
spoken." With that same spirit of faith
we also believe, and therefore speak.
—11 Corinthians 4:13 NIV*

We now conclude with a very important
chapter of this section, "Speaking Blood,
Speaking Faith."

We have learned the blood of Jesus Christ
is alive and speaks today on our behalf. We
have the direct statement in Hebrews:

> *²⁴The blood of sprinkling that speaketh
> better things.* (Hebrews 12:24)

The *"better things"* are the redemption,
forgiveness, cleansing, and such that we
showed to be directly linked to the blood of
Jesus Christ. We discussed in some detail these
examples of *"better things"* which are ours as
New Testament Christians because of the shed
blood.

213

Next, we saw what it meant to apply the blood and to "plead the blood" by the analogy of the Old Testament account of the Passover.

And finally, we showed what it means for us to "plead the blood" to overcome the devil by the *"word of our testimony."*

Now comes the easy-to-say, but hard-to-do part. Our text verse says the bottom line very well, *"We also believe, and therefore speak."*

Let me paraphrase this verse so that I may make my point in the context of the title of this section, "Speaking Blood, Speaking Faith":

> We believe the blood of Jesus Christ is alive, that it speaks on our behalf, and that it has power to overcome the devil when we use it in our testimony against him. We believe this and therefore speak our faith in the blood.

If we believe but don't speak, what good is it? James said a similar thing this way:

> [14]*What doth it profit, my brethren, though a man say he hath faith, and have not works? Can faith save him?*
> [17]*Even so faith, if it hath not works, is dead, being alone.*
> [18]*Yea, a man may say, Thou hast faith, and I have works: show me thy faith without thy works, and I will show thee my faith by my works.*
> (James 2:14, 17-18)

We may believe (have faith) in the living blood, but if we don't exercise our belief (faith), what good is it? Notice verse 18 says the same thing in reverse: *"I will show you my faith by my works."* A paraphrase would be, "I will show you my faith in the blood of Jesus Christ by my speaking its benefits forth." Or, in line with the title of this section, another paraphrase would say, "I will show you my faith in the speaking blood by my speaking faith."

Speaking Faith

We now **know** what it means to "plead the blood." We must now **exercise** that knowledge to make its power operational in our lives.

My suggestion is to begin immediately to memorize and apply the Scriptures that the blood is speaking on our behalf. For example, for the blood-bought provision of our salvation, memorize Ephesians 1:7, *"In him we have redemption through his blood."* When the forces of darkness challenge your salvation, quote this Scripture out loud. Personalize it. Say, "Satan, I have been redeemed by the blood of Jesus Christ." The blood is speaking it; we add our voice, by faith, to speak the same thing.

When unholy thoughts enter the battle ground of your mind, quote Hebrews 13:12 (NIV), *"Jesus also suffered...to make the people holy through his own blood."* Personalize it, out loud, as "I have been made holy by the blood of Jesus." Add something like:

> Satan, the blood of the Lamb overcomes you, and I add the word of my testimony that I have been made holy by the blood of Jesus Christ. Therefore, I will not entertain your unholy thoughts any longer.

The blood is speaking. We are to believe this and speak also. We have the sure word of the Scriptures to activate our faith:

> [24]*The blood of sprinkling that speaketh better things.* (Hebrews 12:24)

> [13]*We also believe, and therefore speak.* (11 Corinthians 4:13)

Speak your faith in the shed blood of Jesus. It is speaking for you!

Chapter 18

By The Blood Of Jesus I Am...

REDEEMED!

> [7]*We have redemption through his blood.*
> *(Ephesians 1:7; Colossians 1:14)*

> [12]*By his own blood he entered in once into the holy place, having obtained eternal redemption for us.* *(Hebrews 9:12)*

> [18]*Ye were...redeemed...*
> [19]*with the precious blood of Christ.*
> *(1 Peter 1:18-19)*

> [9]*Thou...hast redeemed us to God by thy blood.* *(Revelation 5:9)*

FORGIVEN!

> [22]*Without the shedding of blood there is no forgiveness.* *(Hebrews 9:22 NIV)*

*[14]We have redemption through his blood,
the forgiveness of sins.*
(Ephesians 1:7; Colossians 1:14)

CLEANSED!

*[7]The blood of Jesus Christ his Son
cleanseth us from all sin.   (1 John 1:7)*

*[14]The blood of Christ...purge [cleanse] your
conscience from dead works to serve the
living God.   (Hebrews 9:14)*

*[5]Unto him that loved us, and washed
[cleansed] us from our sins in his own
blood.   (Revelation 1:5)*

JUSTIFIED!

*[9]We have now been justified [acquitted] by
his blood.   (Romans 5:9 NIV)*

RECONCILED!

*[25]For God set him before the world, to be,
by the shedding of his blood, a means of
reconciliation through faith.*
(Romans 3:25 TCNT)

20Through him to reconcile to himself all things...by making peace through his blood, shed on the cross.
                              (Colossians 1:20 NIV)

SANCTIFIED!

29The blood of the covenant that sanctified him.   *(Hebrews 10:29 NIV)*

12Jesus also suffered...to make the people holy [sanctified] through his own blood.
                              (Hebrews 13:12 NIV)

PEACEFUL!

20And, having made peace through the blood of his cross...   *(Colossians 1:20)*

BOLD TO APPROACH GOD!

19Having...boldness to enter into the holiest by the blood of Jesus.
                              (Hebrews 10:19)

13Now in Christ Jesus you who were once far away have been brought near through the blood of Christ.
                              (Ephesians 2:13 NIV)

GIVEN ETERNAL INHERITANCE!

[12][Christ]...by his own blood...obtained eternal redemption for us...
[15]that they which are called might receive the promise of eternal inheritance.
(Hebrews 9:12, 15)

PURGED!

[14]How much more shall the blood of Christ...purge your conscience from dead works to serve the living God?
(Hebrews 9:14)

SPRINKLED!

[24]The sprinkled blood that speaks a better word than the blood of Abel.
(Hebrews 12:24 NIV)
[2]To obey Jesus Christ and be sprinkled with his blood. *(1 Peter 1:2 MOFFAT)*

HEALED!

[24]By whose stripes ye were healed.
(1 Peter 2:24 KJV)

24His bruising was your healing.
(1 Peter 2:24 TCNT)

24By his wounds you have been healed.
(1 Peter 2:24 NEB)

24It was the suffering that he bore which has healed you.   (1 Peter 2:24 PHILLIPS)

AN OVERCOMER!

11They overcame him by the blood of the Lamb, and by the word of their testimony.
(Revelation 12:11)

Bibliography

Chambers, Oswald, *God's Workmanship,* as quoted in *Oswald Chambers, the Best from All His Books.* Nashville, TN: Oliver Nelson, 1984.

Frodsham, Stanley H., Preface to *The Power of the Blood,* by H. A. Maxwell Whyte. Springdale, PA: Whitaker House, 1973.

Martin, Ralph P., *New Testament Foundations,* Vol. 2. Grand Rapids, MI: Eerdmans, 1958.

Murray, Andrew, *The Power of the Blood of Jesus.* Springdale, PA: Whitaker House, 1993.

Nee, Watchman, *The Better Covenant.* New York, NY: Christian Fellowship Publishers, 1982.

Schoch, David, *Transcribed Sermon of October 11, 1964.* Long Beach, CA: Bethany Chapel, 1964.

Sumrall, Lester, *Deliverance Class: Tape Recording of May 12, 1980.* South Bend, IN: Lester Sumrall Evangelistic Association, 1980.

Thiessen, Henry C., *Lectures in Systematic Theology.* Grand Rapids, MI: Eerdmans, 1949.

Trumbull, H. Clay, *The Blood Covenant.* Kirkwood, MO: Impact Books, 1975.

Vine, W. E., *An Expository Dictionary of New Testament Words.* Old Tappan, NJ: Revell, 1966.

Williams, Brian, *The Holy Communion.* Birmingham, UK: Brian Williams Evangelistic Association, 1964.

Whyte, H. A. Maxwell, *The Power of the Blood.* Springdale, PA: Whitaker House, 1973.